CHASING SMOKE

COOKING OVER FIRE AROUND THE LEVANT

SARIT PACKER AND ITAMAR SRULOVICH

CHASING SMOKE

COOKING OVER FIRE AROUND THE LEVANT

SARIT PACKER AND ITAMAR SRULOVICH

PAVILION

Honey & Co.

First published in the United Kingdom in 2021
by Pavilion
43 Great Ormond Street
London
WC1N 3HZ

Copyright © Pavilion Books Company Ltd 2021
Text copyright © Saritamar Media Ltd 2021
Photography © Patricia Niven 2021
Cover photography

ISBN 978-1-911641-32-2

A CIP catalogue record for this book is available
from the British Library.

10 9 8 7 6 5 4 3

www.pavilionbooks.com

Reproduction by Mission
Printed and bound by Toppan Leefung Printing
Ltd, China

Publisher: Helen Lewis
Editors: Cara Armstrong and Elizabeth Hallett
Copyeditor: Bryony Nowell
Design: Dave Brown
Photography: Patricia Niven
Production Controller: Phil Brown

Chasing Smoke

Mustafa was waiting for us at Cairo International Airport to take us to our hotel downtown. We had thought about renting a car, but negotiating the streets of Cairo is not something any visitor should attempt, so we put our trust in Mustafa, driver and self-appointed tour guide. As we hit a three-lane road with five rows of cars squeezed door-to-door and bumper-to-bumper, a scattering of scooters and the occasional horse cart inching forward in the afternoon traffic, the air is thick with desert dust and smog, a thousand car horns and *muezzins* calling people to *salat-al-maghrib*, the evening prayer.

Deft as a dancer, brave as a bullfighter and with the faith of a poker player, Mustafa takes these roads without breaking a sweat, while we curl with terror and excitement in the back seat. We nearly scream when the car stops just shy of hitting a pedestrian, who appears out of nowhere in the packed road, but Mustafa explains that the only way to cross a road in Cairo is to go for it and hope for the best. It usually works. The car ahead of us has its boot open; two children sit with their legs dangling out and hands over their heads, keeping the lid from slamming closed. They squeal with joy and fear as if it's the best rollercoaster

ride ever, waving at us and making faces. As Mustafa overtakes, we try to count the number of people inside – four heads in the back (but there may be more), one squashed against the glass, while in the front seat a plump man and his smiling wife cradle a child across their knees.

Buses ride with their doors open, rather than pull up to the kerb, so people can pop in and out. A guy with a vegetable truck is doing brisk trade as commuters nip out of their cars or the bus to get provisions, suddenly rushing back as the traffic starts to move. Mustafa sees this slow, hair-raising journey as an opportunity to point out the sights – the Citadel and Alabaster Mosque, with the neat neighbourhood of *al Arafa* at their feet, the City of the Dead. Even when his knowledge is patchy, he still finds something to say: "See these statues? Famous people from the past." He swerves to avoid a couple of drivers who have left their vehicles and started yelling at each other. "Nothing to worry about," he says. "People think the Cairenes are always shouting but this is just how we talk. It doesn't mean that they're going to start a fight." Pretty soon the drivers start roughing each other up. "Don't even worry about it," he shrugs. "It's not serious until there are more than

two people involved." Just as we drive by, other people leave their cars to join the mêlée. We are transfixed, looking through the back window till Mustafa calls, "Look, you can see the tips of the pyramids!" We're not sure we can, but something else has caught our attention: in the dusty, dusk half-light we are passing a street lit by neon shop signs, and the most delicious-smelling smoke wafts from the grills that line it. "This is *hawawshi* street," Mustafa informs us. "All of Cairo comes here to eat *hawawshi*. Are you hungry?" We don't know what *hawawshi* is, but we are certainly hungry from our flight and hungry for a taste of this city, so Mustafa stops the car.

The street is buzzing with people. All the shops here sell the same dish, but Mustafa knows which one is best, so this is the one we go to. The grill guys are on autopilot, working at full speed. They take a big *baladi* flatbread, slice it open, fill it with minced meat, cheese and sliced chilli peppers, close it and grill it till the meat is cooked, the cheese melted and the bread (which has been brushed with clarified butter) is a crisp, delicious shell. These golden discs come fresh and hot from the grill, a cross between a pizza and a burger, but so much better than either.

There's a little pot of pickles and another of tahini, and we sit at a table on a side street, dipping our wedges of *hawawshi*, while Mustafa shows us pictures of him and his son, a giant perch they caught in the Nile, and the lemon tree in his backyard. We tell him that we want to go to Alexandria and his face lights up. "Alexandria! *Arouset el bahr*, the bride of the sea, the mermaid, so beautiful. The food is so nice, restaurants on the beach, beautiful! You will love it! The old city is quite small so you can walk everywhere," he says, "which is good, because the traffic there is really bad."

It is dark now and the streets have a different feel, quieter, less hectic. Further down the street we see a glow and smell fresh bread; it's the bakery where they make the *baladi* bread we just ate. They are lighting the wood oven in preparation for baking all night. Mustafa says, "Wanna see?"

That trail of smoke is one we have been following all our lives. From Haifa and Jerusalem where we grew up, throughout our travels around the Mediterranean, it has led us to rooftops in Marrakesh, to beach shacks in Kefalonia, and to London's Lebanese restaurants on the Edgware Road and the Turkish kebab shops on Green Lanes. We have learned that good things await us at the end of that trail: where there's smoke, there is fire, and where there's fire, there are often people and stories and something good cooking. Where there's fire, food, friendships and memories are made.

Our own fire burns at the northern end of Great Portland Street in London, in our grill house Honey & Smoke. Every morning our grill is stacked with coal and wood, then lit. Aubergines, squashes, courgettes and onions are charred for salads and sides, and all the good gossip is dished. Lamb is marinated in sage and lemon rind; octopus is braised to soft submission before it goes on the blazing coals; prawns are threaded on skewers; and the drama of our life in the kitchen plays out. Everywhere we've been, all the food we've tried on our travels, and all the people that we've met along the way – all are in our restaurant. Every morning when we light up the grill, we go on another adventure.

We hope our fire sends a wisp of smoke out to the street, and that people – chefs, waiters, guests – follow the trail just as we do. When you get to us, we hope you find something good to eat and join us, either in the restaurant or through this book, on a sunny Middle Eastern journey.

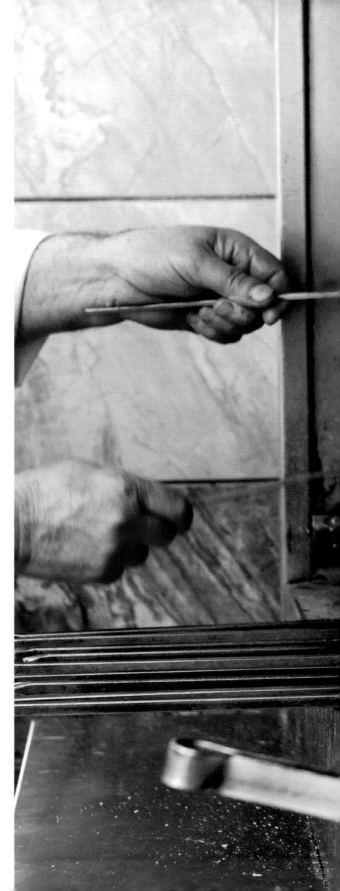

INTRODUCTION

How to BBQ

I grew up in a very English household in the middle of a completely different culture. My parents emigrated to Israel in 1970, before I was born, and decided to make their life and raise their kids there. In some ways they remained very British. In others they embraced the Levant and its customs, most notably the weekend tradition of grilling food outside and eating with your fingers.

We used to call my father a pyromaniac; his idea of fun was gardening (a very British pastime) and burning all the garden waste in a fire pit in the backyard (a typically local thing to do), before lighting the BBQ to cook lunch or dinner. My mum would prepare oblong silver trays of raw chops, steak, kebabs or chicken and send them out to him, with some salt, pepper and the ubiquitous 'chicken grill spice' (a powder made mostly of paprika and MSG – delicious). My job was to take the trays out to my dad along with a little dish containing oil and half an onion to clean the grill, and hand him a beer or a shandy.

As each batch of meat was cooked, I would take it back to the kitchen where my mum would pop it in the oven on a very low heat to keep warm, away from the flies, the cats, and us children, who were driven mad by the delicious smell.

Once all the meat was cooked, we could finally sit down to eat. There would always be a wide selection of salads, some home-made, others shop-bought – a potato salad or a Russian salad, cabbage in some form, a huge bowl of chopped vegetables – and of course hummus, BBQ sauce, and plenty of fresh pitta to mop everything up. We would attack with enthusiasm, and within minutes there would be little left to show for all the work apart from our sticky fingers and messy faces.

The reason I am writing this is not to claim that I picked up BBQ tongs at the age of 8 and became a world-famous grill chef, but rather to say that, as a child, I never did anything more than ferry a platter from one place to another. I never looked at how my father actually started the fire, or how he judged when it was time to start grilling, or how he knew when the meat was cooked. To be honest, I am still not sure how he knew. He can make a decent dinner in the kitchen but it is not his hobby or his passion and, even in this age of smashing the patriarchy, my mum, sister and I actually did most of the cooking.

So how did he know what to do? Maybe there is something instinctive in all of us, a primal sense that kicks in when we place raw food on a grill, telling us how it should smell, when to turn it, when it is cooked. Maybe it was years of experience, of trial and error, that made fire-cooking natural to him. Maybe when he first started grilling, my parents only ate burnt food. Who knows? Luckily for me, by the time I came along he was pretty much an expert and the food was always delicious.

When we decided to open a grill restaurant in London, I was unsure of myself. My husband had been driving me crazy about the idea for years, saying that this was the way forward (which was surprising to me, as it felt more like looking backwards to the earliest, primal form of cooking, a world away from fancy machines with built-in thermometers and gauges). I had been a chef for nearly 20 years, working in many different kitchens, and running our own little restaurant for five years, and yet I wasn't even sure I knew how to start a fire. I assumed that Honey & Smoke would be Itamar's domain, and that I would stay at Honey & Co, safe in my comfort zone.

Of course, reality always differs from the plan. As soon as we had installed our very expensive extraction system and our lovely grill, I simply couldn't stay away. Once you've learned how to light and mellow the grill, cooking on fire is exactly like cooking on the stove, but the flavours are so much greater. Perhaps surprisingly, it is vegetables that benefit most from a bit of grilling; the smoke penetrates and intensifies them, and the results are simply delicious.

Whether you are a bit of a pyromaniac who has been happily grilling over flame for years, or a competent cook who has never even started a BBQ, the recipes in this book can easily make cooking with fire a part of your day-to-day life. For tips on how to light and manage your BBQ, see page 235.

Basic instructions – the way we work

Weights In recipes where it matters, I have stated the net weight of the prepared vegetables and fruits for guidance.

Ingredients Each chapter starts with a little introduction to the main ingredients. I suggest you read these before you shop.

Nuts and seeds We use a lot of nuts and seeds, and the recipe will always state whether they should be roasted or not. If you are roasting them yourself, you can either use the oven or a frying pan on the stove top or BBQ. To oven-roast, lay the nuts or seeds on a baking tray and place in the centre of the oven at 190°C/170°C fan/gas mark 5. Check them every 4–5 minutes, stirring each time, and cook until they are golden (seeds will take about 10 minutes; nuts about 12–15 minutes). If they have their skins on, split one in half to check the colour inside. To pan-roast, put the nuts or seeds in a dry frying pan, metal colander or sieve, and set on the low-heat zone of your BBQ. Shake the pan every few seconds and remove from the heat once they are golden. This method requires more attention than oven-roasting, but if you already have the fire lit, you might as well make the most of it.

Garlic We always use fresh garlic and not pre-minced, as the flavour changes when it has been sitting around for too long.

Lemon juice We use freshly-squeezed lemon juice for the same reason.

General preparation Please read the entire recipe before you start cooking, or indeed shopping. Always good practice.

Fire safety All the recipes in this book are designed to be cooked over a live fire. I am not your mother or babysitter, but please be careful, as it can be really dangerous. Keep bottles of oil or other flammable materials away from the fire, and most importantly, keep kids and pets away too. Make sure you have everything you need before you head outside, so that you can be calm and collected when cooking. Remember that it is better to burn the food than a limb, so don't ever stick your fingers in the fire. Finally, if you are grilling in an open space, always make sure the fire is out before you leave.

A note on brines and salt rubs

Smoking and cooking meat, poultry and fish over fire can really dry them out. One of the best ways to keep them moist (and add seasoning before cooking) is to use a salt rub or a brine. Several dishes in this book set out precise combinations of salt and aromatics to be used, but the general method is worth learning and experimenting with, so that you can apply it to whatever you end up cooking on the BBQ.

Wet brines

The rule of thumb is:

1 heaped tbsp salt for every 250 ml / 8¾ fl oz boiling water

aromatics – hardy herbs (e.g. thyme, rosemary, bay, sage) and/or whole spices (e.g. coriander seeds, fennel seeds, black peppercorns)

a few slices of citrus or garlic cloves (if you like)

Dissolve the salt in the hot water, then add whatever aromatics you fancy along with any garlic and/or lemon. Cool the solution in the fridge before using.

The brining time will vary depending on the size, cut and type of food you are preparing, but whatever it is, it must be fully submerged. A chicken or duck breast, or a whole fish, will only need 20–30 minutes, whereas a whole bird or a big hunk of meat can do with up to 24 hours. Remove from the brining solution and pat dry before grilling.

Salt rubs (dry brines)

There are two main types of salt rub; one contains sugar for a sweet, sticky result; the other is purely an aromatic salt. Both types infuse the food with your chosen flavours before you even start cooking. Whichever type you are using, sprinkle delicately all over, and make sure that you rub it into the whole fish, poultry or meat. Cover and place in the fridge to rest and absorb the flavours for up to 12 hours, depending on the piece. Dab dry before grilling.

Sweet salt rubs

These tend to contain twice as much sugar as salt, as well as lots of warming ground spices. Try the following rub on a rack of beef short ribs, allowing at least 6 hours (and up to 24 hours) for the flavours to develop before grilling.

200 g / 7 oz dark brown sugar

100 g / 3½ oz flaky sea salt

1 tsp freshly ground black pepper

1 tsp ground cumin

1 tsp ground cinnamon

1 tsp ground (allspice) pimento

Aromatic salt rub

These involve lots of pounded herbs, citrus zest and/or chilli. Try this one on a whole side of salmon, pounding the ingredients together with a mortar and pestle, rubbing it on the fish, and then resting it covered in the fridge for a couple of hours.

2 tbsp flaky sea salt

zest of 1 lemon

5 cm / 2 inch piece of fresh ginger, grated

1 small bunch of thyme, leaves picked

Fruit & Vegetables

We love food markets, and never feel that we have really got to know a place until we have found the market and rummaged around the stalls, sniffing fruit and fresh herbs, squeezing vegetables, checking out the local pickling customs and exploring a new food culture. Of course, not everyone will think that a holiday should be spent in the market, with the noise, smells and rough-and-ready nature of such places, but we adore the vibrant life we generally find there.

There is nothing quite like recently harvested vegetables and fruits that have been brought straight to market; they still have the lovely smell of the field or tree where they were picked. As we walk around the stalls, we let our noses lead the way. When we smell something super-fresh, we know we should buy that bunch of parsley or coriander; a zingy smell usually leads us to the best lemons or freshest ginger;

and just a whiff of earthy richness has us running to the beetroot stall, rubbing speckles of mud off the bulbs to see the purple skin beneath. It is all part of the experience.

We try to buy and eat seasonally, as the flavours are so much better, and honestly, one of the best things about travelling is visiting those markets that keep the tradition of only selling what is in season. Green almonds appear for just one month a year; figs are a cause for celebration when they arrive; and strawberries, well, they always remind me of my birthday and the start of the Mediterranean winter, awakening the excitement I felt as a child.

In the Levant, grilling vegetables is often about getting as much flavour as you can into those veggies which have to be cooked and need an extra lift – potatoes, corn, aubergines, artichokes – the usual suspects. They taste great when baked in the embers or charred

over a flaming grill and, with the addition of a sauce or dressing, can make a meal on their own.

Grilling really works its magic on unlikely vegetables and fruits. Add a touch of smoke to young courgettes with their flowers still attached, dress them with some fresh grapes and yogurt, and suddenly they become something truly special. Griddle ripe peaches or soft, succulent figs and you can use them to create decadent salads that are true show-stoppers.

Don't limit yourself to grilling on a summer's afternoon. Try lighting the BBQ on an autumn or winter evening and grilling some chestnuts, apples and pumpkins. Cooking over glowing coals will transform the way you see fruits and vegetables, and the fire will keep you warm on a chilly night.

FRUIT & VEGETABLES

London, England: 216 Great Portland Street

A big, square room, white walls, neon lights, plastic chairs and Formica-topped tables set with napkin dispensers and cutlery in jars. The service is friendly but curt. The menus are laminated but nobody looks at them, as everyone comes here for the grilled chicken. The waiter just wants to know how much of it you'd like.

This is Nimer Restaurant in northern Israel. Sarit's family has been coming here for years and we came together early in our relationship, when we were introducing each other to our favourite eateries. The table filled up with the usual mezze and stacks of fresh bread; the famous chicken came sizzling from the grill, charred and juicy. We talked about the skills required to pull a bird off the heat at just the right moment, and how this and places like this are exactly what we enjoy: buzzing, welcoming and egalitarian; not fancy, never painful, just delicious, easy fun. That night, that conversation started us on a decade-long journey to many such places around the world, from Marrakesh to Istanbul, a journey that led us to Honey & Smoke.

In late 2014 we were looking for a place to open our own grill house. It had to be big enough for a proper kitchen and preferably no more than five minutes' walk from Honey & Co, our first restaurant. We were shown a shop in Great Portland Street which was way too big and expensive, but we had no choice – it was perfect. A tile showroom on a main road, it needed to be converted to become a restaurant, which meant zoning applications and expensive building work, but it also meant we could have the kitchen exactly as we wanted.

Negotiating the contract took two years, and the resulting agreement allows our satanic landlords to harvest our organs at will. The fit-out took a nerve-wrecking six months, in which the builders had to dig down three metres for the drains and build up fifteen metres to install the extractor system, but when they finally left we had a neon-lit room with a hundred plastic chairs set at laminated tables, a shiny new kitchen with bright yellow floors, a state-of-the-art bakery, plenty of fridge space and, at the restaurant's heart, the grill of our dreams, now a reality.

While a dream is a fixed idea, and somewhat rose-tinted, reality is ever-changing, evolving and complex. The place was busy from the moment we opened the door and has only got busier with time. With just the two of us in the kitchen at the start, we had to adapt quickly to the demands of a busy hundred-seater restaurant. As people joined us, they had an impact on our offering: for a long time we had a big Greek contingent who introduced *gyros* to the menu, while our Argentinian head chef Maria Paz brought her discerning palate and imagination to many of the dishes we now serve.

It turned out that nobody but us liked the neon lights and the plastic chairs, so they went at the first opportunity, but we have always made sure there is the warmest of welcomes. Our ideas of what the menu should be have changed as well. The early notion of meat-stick-fire felt a bit limiting when so many beautiful vegetables and fruits entered our kitchen with the ebb and flow of the seasons, all taking so kindly to the heat and smoke of our grill.

What started out as a dream of a Middle Eastern eatery ended up being a very London restaurant: a crossroads of cultures, a meeting place of old and new, traditional and contemporary. Like London it is influenced by the movement of people and goods, and a commitment to having a good time and a good dinner. But the smell of smoke, the sizzle of the grill and the glow of the embers, warm and lambent, the promise of tasty food and fun times – the things that remind us of Nimer and countless other places like it – are always there.

FRUIT & VEGETABLES

FRUIT & VEGETABLES

Whole burnt aubergine with charred egg yolk, tahini and chilli sauce

Serves 2 as a meal

This is the essence of our food, distilled into a single dish. It is inspired by the first whole burnt aubergine we ever ate, served with a smattering of grated tomato, at a very famous Jerusalem establishment we both love. It has since become a staple at every BBQ, and in our restaurant Honey & Smoke. Burning the aubergine really brings out the best in this slightly bland vegetable. Don't hold back – by the time you're done, the skin should be blackened and the flesh so soft it can easily be scooped out with a spoon.

2 aubergines

50 g / 1¾ oz tahini paste

50 ml / 1¾ fl oz ice-cold water

2 egg yolks from beautiful eggs

For the lemon, chilli and garlic dressing

1 red chilli, deseeded and finely chopped (about 10 g / ⅓ oz)

1 green chilli, deseeded and finely chopped (about 10 g / ⅓ oz)

3 large garlic cloves, peeled and finely chopped (about 20 g / ¾ oz)

juice of 1–2 lemons (about 80 ml / 2¾ fl oz)

1 tsp table salt

1 tsp ground cumin

1 tsp caster sugar

2 tbsp olive oil

1 bunch of parsley, leaves picked and chopped (about 30 g / 1 oz)

Place the whole aubergines on a very hot grill, or directly on the embers if you prefer. Let them scorch all over, turning occasionally, until the skin is charred and the flesh is so soft that it seems they are going to collapse.

While the aubergines are cooking, combine all the dressing ingredients apart from the chopped parsley. Separately mix the tahini paste with the water to form a thick whipped cream consistency.

Once the aubergines are fully blackened, remove from the grill onto serving plates and slit open to reveal the flesh.

Add the parsley to the dressing and mix well. Use half the dressing to douse the flesh of the slit aubergines, then top with the whipped tahini. Use the back of a spoon to create a little well in the tahini and place a raw egg yolk in the centre of each one. Using tongs, carefully remove a hot charcoal from the fire and lightly char the top of each yolk. Return the coal to the fire and drizzle the remaining dressing over the aubergines before serving.

To cook without a BBQ

Cook the aubergines on your highest grill setting or in a super-hot oven at 240°C/220°C fan/gas mark 9, remembering to pierce them with a fork beforehand, as they have a tendency to explode. Scorch one side, then rotate and char the next section until the flesh of the aubergine is completely soft. Use a blow torch to scorch the surface of the egg yolk, or simply heat the back of a spoon over a flame and use that instead.

Smoky aubergines with tomato and *labaneh*

Serves 4 as a starter

You will need to start preparing the *labaneh* a day before you want to serve this dish, as it needs time to drain overnight. *Labaneh* is a staple in our house and in our restaurants, where there is always a huge batch hanging somewhere. While you may not want to prepare quite as much as we do, I always suggest making a much larger quantity than you need for this recipe, as it keeps well for at least 10 days in the fridge. Use it as a great sandwich filler, or sprinkle with olive oil and *za'atar* for the best dip ever.

2 aubergines (about 300–400g / 10½–14 oz each)
200 g / 7 oz large plum or vine tomatoes
1 tbsp olive oil
2 tbsp red wine vinegar
a generous pinch of flaky sea salt, plus more to serve

For the *labaneh* (to yield 200 g / 7 oz)

400 g / 14 oz full fat Greek-style yogurt
100 g / 3½ oz sour cream
¼ tsp table salt
1 garlic clove, peeled and crushed
2 tbsp olive oil
2 tbsp lemon juice

Mix all the ingredients for the *labaneh* together. Tip into a piece of muslin or cheesecloth and hang over a bowl at room temperature overnight until most of the liquid has drained out, leaving a lovely thick-set yogurt spread. You can now scoop the *labaneh* into a small bowl and set it in the fridge to chill until you are ready to serve.

Place the aubergines on a very hot fire and grill till they are completely soft, rotating them occasionally. You want the skin to really char and the flesh to soften and almost melt away.

Halve the tomatoes and grate the cut surface on the coarse side of a box grater until you are just left with the tomato skin, which you can then discard. If the grated pulp is very watery, you can strain it for a few seconds; if it is very fleshy, leave it as is. You should end up with about 150 g / 5¼ oz pulp. Season it with the olive oil, vinegar and salt, and refrigerate to chill fully.

Slit the charred skin of the aubergines and scoop out the flesh. Spoon the *labaneh* onto a serving plate and top with the aubergine flesh. Drizzle with the tomato dressing, sprinkle with some flaky sea salt and serve.

To cook without a BBQ

You can burn the aubergines directly on the gas flame or use a grill setting on maximum to char and cook them, but nothing tastes quite as good as aubergines cooked over a fire.

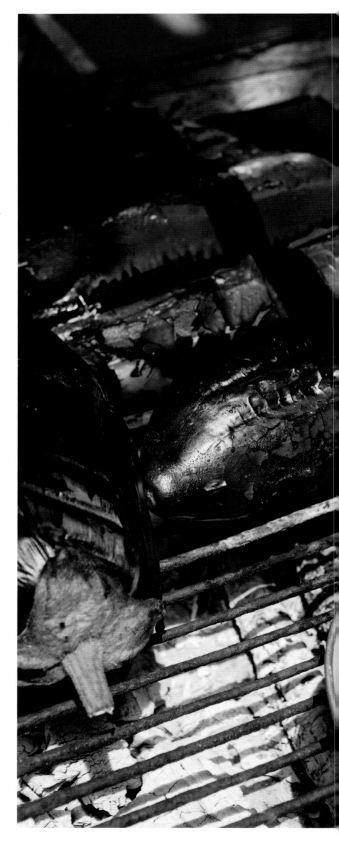

Charred kohlrabi, radish and sesame salad

Serves 4–6 as a side

Kohlrabi is a great vegetable and worth seeking out. This lovely, alien-looking member of the cabbage family is very easy to peel and cook. It is often eaten raw as a simple snack or chopped in salads (I think of it as a savoury apple) but also works well pickled, stuffed or cooked in a stew. If you can't find any, then use thick broccoli stems instead – simply peel, then treat the heart as a delicious vegetable in its own right. If using broccoli stems, you will need at least eight to make this salad.

4 kohlrabi

8–10 radishes

30 g / 1 oz sesame seeds

flaky salt to taste

1 lemon, peeled and divided in segments

1 tsp toasted sesame oil

a small handful of chopped coriander

2 tbsp vegetable oil

Place the whole kohlrabi in the embers of the fire and cook, rotating occasionally, until the skin is black and a knife can be easily inserted into the centre; this will take about 30 minutes. Remove from the fire and cool until you can easily handle them, then peel off the charred black skin. Cut into quarters and slice. Then slice the radishes very thinly.

Toast the sesame seeds in a dry pan on the low-heat zone of your BBQ for 6–8 minutes. Shake the pan every few seconds and remove from the heat once they are golden.

Place the kohlrabi and radishes in a bowl with a good pinch of salt and toss to soften. Add all the other ingredients, mix well, and season with a little extra salt if needed before serving.

To cook without a BBQ

Sprinkle a thin layer of salt in a roasting tin, place the whole unpeeled and unwrapped kohlrabi on top and pop into the oven at 220°C/200°C fan/gas mark 7 for 30–40 minutes until soft.

Grilled cabbage with chilli garlic butter

To serve 4 as a starter or 8 as a side

There is nothing like a market stall piled high with cabbages in a huge variety of shades from pure white to bright lime green or deep purplish red. Some may be larger than your head, their huge leaves used for stuffing; some may be small and crunchy and perfect for salad; some may be more fibrous, lending themselves to slow stewing. White cabbage is possibly the most underrated of all, but we absolutely love it. This is hands down the best way to eat any cabbage. You don't even really need the dressing if you don't fancy it – just grill a cabbage and eat it.

1 large, round white cabbage

2 tbsp olive oil

flaky sea salt

For the dressing

2 banana shallots, peeled and finely chopped

2 red chillies, halved, deseeded and thinly sliced

6 garlic cloves, peeled and minced

100 g / 3½ oz butter

1 tsp flaky sea salt

1 small bunch of dill, fronds roughly chopped

Cut the cabbage into four or six wedges, depending on how large it is, and brush the cut surfaces with olive oil. Set the wedges cut-side down on a very hot grill to char for 4 minutes, then flip and grill the other cut surface for 4 minutes. Finally set the wedges on their rounded sides for a final 4 minutes, just to soften the cabbage a little. Remove to a platter and sprinkle with a little flaky sea salt.

While the cabbage is charring, combine the shallots, chilli and garlic with the butter and set in a small pan on the side of the grill over a low-moderate heat, enough to just melt the butter and lightly confit the vegetables. Stir occasionally, cooking for about 12–14 minutes or until the shallots are soft and look translucent. Remove from the heat, add the salt and chopped dill and mix well. Pour the butter dressing all over the warm cabbage and serve straight away for best results.

To cook without a BBQ

Use a lightly oiled, preheated griddle pan on your stove top and cook the cabbage wedges just as you would on the fire. Prepare the dressing on your stove too, in a small pan over a low heat.

FRUIT & VEGETABLES

Ash-baked beetroot, lentil and feta salad

**A large salad to serve at a party,
or to feed 8–10 as part of a meal**

This dish, created by Maria Paz (who also runs the kitchen), is one of the most popular mezze we serve at Honey & Smoke during the winter months. It makes the most of the earthy beetroots, which combine with the lentils and herbs to create a vibrant, delicious salad.

6–8 beetroots, depending on size (about 1 kg / 2 lb 4 oz)

200 g / 7 oz celery, thinly sliced

1 bunch of dill, fronds roughly chopped (about 30 g / 1 oz)

1 bunch of parsley, leaves picked and roughly chopped (about 30 g / 1 oz)

100 g / 3½ oz crumbled feta

For the pickled onion

80 ml / 2¾ fl oz red wine vinegar

40 ml / 8 tsp water

20 g / ¾ oz sugar

½ tsp salt

2 bay leaves

2 cloves

1 large red onion (about 150 g / 5¼ oz), peeled and diced

For the lentils

250 g / 9 oz brown or puy lentils

½ red onion

2 stalks of celery

2 bay leaves

1 tsp salt

3 tbsp olive oil

Wrap the unpeeled beetroot individually in aluminium foil and place in the embers of the fire. Leave to cook until a knife or skewer goes in easily, about 40–50 minutes, then remove from the heat to cool before unwrapping them. As soon as you can handle them, peel the beetroot, dice into small cubes and place in a large bowl.

To make the pickled onion, put the vinegar, water, sugar, salt, bay leaves and cloves in a small pan and bring to the boil. Then remove from the heat, add the red onion and leave for at least 30 minutes to allow the flavours to develop.

Wash the lentils well and drain. Place in a pan with plenty of fresh water plus the onion, celery and bay leaves and bring to the boil. Skim the foam, reduce the heat to medium and cook until the lentils are just soft but not falling apart (how long this takes will depend on the type you use, but start checking after about 20 minutes). Drain well then tip onto a baking tray. Spread the lentils out, season with the salt, drizzle with the olive oil, mix well and leave to cool. Once cool enough to handle, pick out and discard the cooked onion, celery stalks and bay leaves, and transfer the lentils to the bowl containing the beetroot.

When you're ready to serve, add the onions and the pickling liquid to the beetroot and lentil mixture and stir well to combine. Mix in the celery, dill and parsley, transfer to a serving dish and top with the crumbled feta.

To cook without a BBQ

Sprinkle a thin layer of salt in a roasting tin, place the unpeeled beetroot on top (no need to wrap them in foil) and pop in the oven at 220°C/200°C fan/gas mark 7 for about 60 minutes until soft. Remove from the tin and, once cooled, peel away the skin so you are left with the soft flesh.

Al Salt, Jordan:
Galayet bandora

On the drive from Amman to Al Salt, Ramzi tells us about a girl he met last night: how sweet she is, what nice manners she has. His green eyes light up under heavy brows, visibly smitten. She is a photographer, he says, but not a very good one. He shows us her work on his phone, desert scenes in black and white; gnarly naked trees. "What is this? It's nothing! Look at the pictures I take – much better!" He shows pictures of himself and his friends on a jeep, tongues out and thumbs up. "Nicer, no?"

Actually he was in Al Salt last night. He took this girl to a restaurant there and now he wants us to try it as well. Al Salt, he explains, was chosen by the Emir in the 1920s to be the capital of Jordan, but the local grandees, fearing that the hustle of government would disturb their tranquil community, kicked him down to Amman. We go to the restaurant, which is in one of the beautiful vaulted stone buildings typical of the town. We share a small breakfast: falafel filled with sweet purple onions, and grilled lambs' liver in a syrupy-sharp pomegranate dressing. The manager laughs when he sees Ramzi for the second day in a row. With impeccable manners he urges us to try more of the food and we wish we could, but there are other places Ramzi wants us to see.

The town of Al Salt is sedate and slightly sleepy, with wide streets clad in creamy stone. The market is cool, clean, shady and calm, and the people there are extremely friendly. An old man cooking pancakes to make into sweet stuffed *atayef* invites us into his shop for a natter and a taste; a lady walking past absentmindedly caresses a dress display on a stall, feeling the quality of the fabric. A father taking his young son for lunch stops to chat to us, just so they can both practise their English. The father is a doctor who studied in Moscow; the son wants to be an architect – when he grows up, he will build the tallest building in Jordan! They invite us to join them for lunch, but we sadly decline. We have other plans.

We are going to cook with Ramzi and are here at the market to shop for ingredients. The veg stalls are laden with the finest produce of the Valley of Jethro, some of the most prized agricultural land in the Middle East: sweet onions with some dirt in their roots; green garlic; early spring tomatoes that are flavourful and quite firm, bright red with yellow patches where the sun has reached. These are perfect for making *galayet bandora*, a dish of tomatoes stewed in olive oil, eaten with the flatbread that is so much loved here in Jordan. It is the food of shepherds and field hands, made to be eaten outdoors, which is where Ramzi most likes to be. He grew up in hectic Amman, and during the week he works as a dental technician there, but on weekends, or whenever else he gets the chance, he loves to be out in nature. South to the desert or north to the verdant hills, he knows this country well. His mum is from Syria, and his father's family came from Palestine in '48, but Ramzi is wholly Jordanian.

On the drive into the hills we stop at a bakery for the last ingredient: plump flatbread with a dainty lace-like pattern, as big as a blanket and just as soft. In the car Ramzi plays us a song by a new band he has discovered, with an Arabic reggae-dubstep beat and words he sings along to… "every land is a holy land, every people are the promised people". We all bop our heads, doing the car-dance till we get to our destination, a small patch of land which belongs to a family friend. It slopes down a hill overlooking the Jordan valley and the hills behind it – of Israel and Palestine. In the early spring it is green here: bright green, new-growth grass dotted with pinks and tiny red anemones, daisies in yellow and white, and thumb-sized irises, that are called black but are actually in many deep shades of purple. Few enjoy this quiet glory with us – the only other person about is a shepherd and his fussy flock. The only building in sight is a shepherd's hut of breeze blocks and corrugated iron. Inside are two simple beds and a fireplace made of tins, with a fire-lighting kit next to it: long matches, some dried branches and a stack of paper – old bills, newspapers, school books. We light a fire outside between two blocks by the wall and place a gilded teapot on it. Tea first, always tea first, so we pick wild sage and *za'atar* leaves (hyssop) from the meadow and set it to brew. While the tea cools a bit in our cups we sit back on our patch of grass, leaning against the wonky hut wall, literally drinking in

our surroundings. The sky is the same sky we grew up under, and the field, the flowers, the smell of the land are all familiar to us from childhood, even though we've never been here before. Ahead of us is the river, the border, and beyond it the country we came from, that Ramzi's family came from.

The preparation of the stew is as simple as can be. We heat a *saj* (a wok-like pan) on our little fire till it's good and hot. Local olive oil goes in, ripe and pungent, followed by onion and garlic in quick succession. Not long after that, in go those good, firm tomatoes and some salt. Stir a bit, cover with a lid and let things happen. Some of the tomatoes will collapse into a sauce, some will stick to the bottom of the pan and char, some will keep their shape and bite. A little stirring but not too much – this is not a sauce but a quick tomato stew. You can make the bread over the fire on an upturned *saj* or do as we did and buy it freshly baked. Tear off pieces and scoop the tomatoes up with it, marvelling at how something so simple can taste so good.

A sweet-scented wind carries the smoke from our fire westwards, across the border, and from the hills on the other side we see another trailing wisp of smoke… a shepherd, a farmer or a hiker maybe, and perhaps cooking a similar meal to ours. Ramzi puts some music on, and we all bop our heads to the dubstep beat.

FRUIT & VEGETABLES

Galayet bandora – tomato stew with green chilli

Serve with plenty of flatbread to soak up the party. This can feed a crowd as part of a spread, or 4 as a meal in its own right

4 tbsp olive oil

2 large Spanish onions, peeled and roughly chopped

6 garlic cloves, peeled and thickly sliced

2 green chillies, thinly sliced (keep the seeds in for a spicier result)

1.5 kg / 3 lb 5 oz tomatoes, the ripest you can find

2 tsp salt

1 tbsp sugar

freshly ground black pepper

Set a large wok directly onto a roaring fire. Add the olive oil, heat for a minute, then tip in the onions and garlic. Stir around to coat well and fry until the onions start to soften, but don't let them colour too much. Add the slices of chilli and the tomatoes, toss to coat in the oil and mix through, then sprinkle with the salt and sugar and stir well. Allow to cook for about 15 minutes, stirring occasionally, until the tomatoes have almost completely broken down. You can cover the wok with a lid to help the process along. Just before serving, add a few good twists of black pepper, stir again and dish up while still piping hot.

To cook without a BBQ

You can cook this on a stove over a super-high heat in a wok or similar large pan, but it won't be the same, so ideally go outside and start a fire to cook it over.

Bamya – smoked okra cooked in a spicy tomato sauce

A side dish for 6–8

400 g / 14 oz small okra

3 tbsp olive oil

1–2 onions, peeled and diced (about 200 g / 7 oz)

1 red chilli, deseeded and thinly sliced

3 slices of lemon

4 garlic cloves, peeled and crushed

1 tsp whole coriander seeds

1 tsp whole cumin seeds

1 tsp salt

4 large tomatoes, roughly diced (about 400 g / 14 oz)

1 tbsp tomato paste

300 ml / 10½ fl oz water

Trim the okra by just nipping the stalks off – don't go too deep as you want them to stay sealed. Place in a large colander, sieve or special smoking tray (if you have one). Once you have lit the fire and it is creating a lot of smoke, place the okra in its container directly over the smokiest part. Leave to infuse and colour a little, tossing the veg around occasionally, until the charcoal has caught properly and settled into nice hot embers (this will take about 10–12 minutes).

Place a frying pan on the heat, pour in the oil, warm it a little, then add the onion and fry for about 4–5 minutes until well coloured. Stir in the chilli and lemon slices along with the garlic (best to step aside to avoid the chilli fumes) and continue to stir until the colours deepen. Make sure the pan is on the hottest part of the grill, add the smoked okra, toss to combine well, then tip in the whole spices and salt, followed by the tomatoes. Continue to cook till the tomatoes break up nicely (about 4–5

minutes). Finally mix in the tomato paste and water, pull the pan to a cooler corner of the grill and leave to cook really slowly until the sauce thickens and the okra is soft (about 20–30 minutes).

To cook without a BBQ

You can cook this on the stove without smoking the okra, and maybe use smoked salt, if you have any, to impart a little of the flavour. It won't be the same, obviously, but it's worth it if you like okra. (If you don't, use flat beans or bobby beans instead.)

Tomato and *kashkaval* salad

A salad for 6–8 as part of a spread

1 kg / 2 lb 4 oz mixed tomatoes of all shapes and sizes

olive oil for brushing, plus 3 tbsp for drizzling

½ tsp sugar

1 tsp salt

2 tbsp red wine vinegar

3 garlic cloves, peeled and thinly sliced

1 green chilli, halved, deseeded and thinly sliced

4 sprigs of fresh oregano, leaves picked

4 sprigs of fresh basil, leaves picked and ripped in half

50 g / 1¾ oz *kashkaval* cheese (or young Pecorino),
thinly shaved with a peeler

Halve all the larger tomatoes, but keep any baby or cherry ones whole. Brush the cut surfaces with olive oil and put the halved tomatoes flat-side down on a very hot grill. Place the whole ones on a fine mesh over the heat too – you could use a wide colander to make sure they don't fall into the fire. Grill until the skins start to explode.

Remove to a large bowl, sprinkle with the sugar and salt, then drizzle with the vinegar. Add the sliced garlic and chilli, and leave to marinate for 10–15 minutes. Transfer to a serving plate, scatter the picked herbs and thinly shaved cheese all over, drizzle with the olive oil and serve.

To cook without a BBQ

Use a lightly oiled, preheated griddle pan on your stove top and cook just as you would on the fire, taking care not to overcrowd the pan – you want the tomatoes to get plenty of heat so that they burst and char.

FRUIT & VEGETABLES

FRUIT & VEGETABLES

Grilled tomato skewers

Makes 4 skewers

4 large San Marzano plum tomatoes
(they are the long firm ones)

12 large sage leaves

1 large red onion, peeled
and quartered

salt and pepper

For the *salsa verde*

1 small bunch of parsley, leaves picked
(about 20 g / ¾ oz)

1 small of bunch basil, leaves picked
(about 20 g / ¾ oz)

3 sprigs of marjoram, leaves picked

1 large garlic clove, peeled
and crushed

zest and juice of 1 lemon

3 tbsp olive oil

salt and pepper to taste

Cut each tomato into three thick slices and slide them onto the skewer alternately with a leaf of sage and a piece of onion. Season well with salt and pepper.

Place cut-side down on a really high heat and cook until coloured, about 2–3 minutes, then flip and continue grilling until all sides have got a good colour to them. Remove to a serving plate.

While the tomatoes are cooking, finely chop the parsley, basil and marjoram leaves and mix with the rest of the *salsa verde* ingredients. Spoon over the warm skewers and serve.

To cook without a BBQ

Use a lightly oiled, preheated griddle pan on your stove top and cook just as you would on the fire (it may be easier to do this without the skewers).

Alexandria, Egypt: Fires on the shore

Centuries ago, when Egypt was a regional superpower, Alexandria was its gateway to Mediterranean trade. Boats sailed by the famous lighthouse, one of the Seven Wonders of the Ancient World. Scholars studying everything from law and medicine to lyric poetry and comedy attended the Great Library. Queen Cleopatra played out her dramatic life in this town; the remains of her palace lie under the water, fish swimming around the drowned sphinxes and fallen urns.

Julius Caesar accidentally destroyed the majority of the library over 2,000 years ago, and the lighthouse is long gone too, although parts remained until the 1400s, when they were finally dismantled and the stones used to build a fort. The great beacon may have disappeared, but smaller fires along the shore still beckon you to moor here for a while. As soon as the setting sun hits the horizon, an army of vendors materializes on the Corniche, the city's breezy seaside promenade. Little fires are built in metal drums and buckets, the coals heated and loaded onto wooden carts, glowing in the growing darkness like fireflies, ready to provide warm refreshments through the sultry city nights. Sunset is the best time to arrive in town: this is *wa'at el habiba*, the time of lovers, and Alexandrians are lovers of the sea; this is their time. Young couples stroll hand in hand; friends walk side by side, elbows locked; families try to keep pace with their young and their old. You too can stroll along the promenade and look at the boats, or sit on the sea wall and watch the world go by. If you get yourself a good bench overlooking the harbour, it could be the hottest table in town – no fancy restaurant view could match the beauty of this city and the sea under a burnt pink sunset.

The culinary offerings are varied and delicious, if simple. Start with a drink. The tea ladies have tiny metal trolleys with small charcoal trays on top for boiling water. Black tea and mint are steeped and sugared to a thick, heady syrup – Alexandrians like it sweet (*mazboot*) or very sweet (*helou*). For *hors d'oeuvres* there are nuts and seeds: freshly-roasted, salted sunflower and pumpkin seeds (a well-loved snack here); lupin seeds and whole almonds in saltwater; hot roasted peanuts in a paper cone, kept piping hot by burning coals in a compartment of the wooden carts, which somehow don't burst into flames.

Main courses are light but extremely satisfying: rickety carts with little in-built braziers dispense sweetcorn, grown in the Nile Delta. Juicy and fresh, grilled with chilli and served with a cheek of lemon (Egyptian lemons are second to none), the combination makes for a startling mouthful as each sweet, hot, sour kernel explodes in your mouth with a pop. Long and thin, heavy and compact, local sweet potatoes are roasted very slowly on coals, constantly turned till their red skin is completely black and their flesh is soft. Wrapped in yesterday's papers, they cost next to nothing and may not seem anything special until the sweet, smoky steam mixed with sea breeze hits your nose and you spoon in that first mouthful, like rich treacle or soft caramel with the crunch of salt crystals as a delicious counterpoint.

There's so much to enjoy here: welcome to Alexandria.

Grilled corn – with 3 serving suggestions

Allow at least one whole corn cob per person

Corn husks carry loads of flavour and it is well worth using them when cooking, even if you are simply boiling the cob in its husk. If you can't get corn with the husks still on, wrap each cob in a sheet of baking paper and then a sheet of aluminium foil to form a little protective jacket – this will help you steam, rather than burn, the kernels at the first stage of cooking.

corn cobs – as many as you want to eat

Place the whole cobs in their husks over a medium heat on the BBQ and allow them to take on plenty of colour, rotating every 3–4 minutes, until they are really charred (15 minutes in total should do the trick). Remove from the heat and set aside for 10 minutes, then pull back most of the burnt husk (or remove the paper and foil wrapper) and return to a very high-heat grill for a minute or two to char some of the flesh really quickly for a lovely smoky flavour and chewy texture. Serve straight away with either or both of the following suggested dressings, or set aside to cool before making a charred corn salad.

To cook without a BBQ

Use a lightly oiled, preheated griddle pan on your stove top and cook just as you would on the fire.

Honey and *urfa* chilli butter

Enough for 4–6 corn cobs

4–6 grilled corn cobs (see left)

80 g / 2¾ oz salted butter

1 tbsp honey

1 tbsp *urfa* chilli flakes

Place a small frying pan on the BBQ, add the butter and melt it until it starts to foam. Remove from the heat, add the honey and *urfa* chilli, and mix well to combine. Return the pan to the heat to foam the butter again, then serve drizzled all over the corn cobs.

Olive oil, garlic and chive dressing

Enough for 4–6 corn cobs

4–6 grilled corn cobs (see left)

3 cloves of garlic

1 small bunch of chives

80 ml / 2¾ fl oz olive oil

½ tsp flaky sea salt

freshly ground black pepper

Peel and mince the garlic, finely chop the chives, then mix with the olive oil and salt, seasoning to taste with freshly ground black pepper. Serve with the grilled corn.

Charred corn salad with coriander, chilli and avocado

4 grilled corn cobs (see left)

2 green chillies

4 spring onions, thinly sliced

2 limes

2 ripe avocados

3 tbsp olive oil

flaky sea salt

freshly ground black pepper

1 small bag of rocket (about 60 g / 2¼ oz), washed

1 bunch of coriander, leaves picked

Use a sharp serrated knife to remove the kernels from the cooked corn cobs, cutting as close to the core of the cob as possible. Place the kernels in a large bowl. Thinly slice the green chillies, keeping the seeds if you want the salad to be very spicy. Add to the bowl along with the spring onions and the juice of one lime. Cut the other lime into quarters and slice each quarter as thinly as you can. Peel and slice the avocados. Place the lime slivers and avocado slices in the bowl, pour in the olive oil and season with salt and pepper. Finally, add the rocket and coriander leaves. Toss gently to mix, then serve immediately at room temperature.

FRUIT & VEGETABLES

Grilled artichokes – 3 ways to cook and 3 dips to serve

All through the Mediterranean you can buy ready-prepared artichoke hearts in market places, making the whole process of grilling them so much easier and more accessible. The hearts are perfectly suited to grilling and they benefit from the smokiness this gives them. If you don't live near a market that sells them ready-trimmed, and the idea of prepping an artichoke down to the heart fills you with dread, then good news: you can just as easily grill them whole or halved (the work of getting into the heart is up to each diner).

Whole

Use globe artichokes or baby violet artichokes – as many as you want to eat

No preparation of the artichokes is needed; simply wrap the stems and bases in aluminium foil so just the tops of the leaves are showing. Place them directly in the embers, stem-side down and leaves pointing up. Leave to cook for approximately 15 minutes for baby artichokes and 30 minutes for whole globe ones, then remove from the fire. As soon as you can handle them, peel away the foil and serve just as they are, with the dips (see page 59) on the side. Each diner should peel the leaves off one by one, scooping a little dip onto the base and scraping each leaf between the teeth to remove the soft section, until the coveted heart is reached. Then they only need to scrape away the choke (the hairy-looking fibres) with a teaspoon, and enjoy the heart with some sea salt and slathered in the dip of their choice.

Halved

Use globe artichokes or baby violet artichokes – as many as you want to eat

Very little preparation is required: simply cut the artichokes in half through the stem and heart and use a teaspoon to scrape away the choke. Rub the cut surfaces all over with half a lemon, then brush with some olive oil and sprinkle with salt. Place the halved artichokes flat-side down on a medium-hot grill for about 12 minutes. Flip them over, brush the flat, charred surface with a little more olive oil and sprinkle with salt while the leaf-side cooks for 10 minutes, then serve alongside the dips (see page 59). You can fill the cavity where the choke was with sauce or dressing and then use a teaspoon to scoop out the flesh from around the heart.

Hearts

Buy a whole load of prepared artichoke hearts (or, of course, prepare your own)

Place the hearts in a large pot of water seasoned with two halved lemons, a small bunch of thyme, a halved head of garlic and a generous amount of salt. Boil for 15 minutes, then drain. Lay the hearts flat on a baking tray, drizzle generously with olive oil, then pop them directly on the grill to char and finish cooking. Serve as they are, with any or all of the dips on page 59.

To cook without a BBQ

Halved or hearts: after the initial preparation set out above, use a lightly oiled, preheated griddle pan on your stove top and cook just as you would on the fire.

FRUIT & VEGETABLES

Wild garlic (ramsons or bear's garlic) mayonnaise

Enough for 4–6

4–8 grilled artichokes or hearts (see page 56), depending on their size

6 wild garlic leaves

1 tbsp white wine vinegar

1 egg yolk

1 tsp Dijon mustard

100 ml / 3½ fl oz vegetable oil

flaky sea salt

freshly ground black pepper

Boil some water and blanch the garlic leaves for 10 seconds before transferring to ice-cold water to cool. Remove from the water, squeeze out any excess liquid and pop the leaves into a food processor. Add the vinegar, egg yolk and mustard and blitz to a smooth purée. With the food processor on a medium setting, slowly drizzle in the oil in a steady stream until it is combined and the mayonnaise has thickened. Season with a pinch of salt and pepper, and blitz one more time.

Preserved lemon and poppy seed salsa

Enough for 4–6

4–8 grilled artichokes or hearts (see page 56), depending on their size

100 g / 3½ oz whole preserved lemons (to produce 50 g / 1¾ oz lemon peels)

100 ml / 3½ fl oz olive oil

1 tbsp poppy seeds

1 small bunch of parsley, leaves picked and chopped

Scoop out and discard all the pulp and seeds from the lemons. Blitz the peels to a rough paste in a food processor then remove to a small bowl. Add the olive oil, poppy seeds and chopped parsley and stir well to combine.

Harissa yogurt dip

Enough for 4–6

4–8 grilled artichokes or hearts (see page 56), depending on their size

250 g / 9 oz full fat yogurt

2 tsp harissa paste

½ tsp ground cumin

1 small clove of garlic, peeled and minced

1 tbsp olive oil

Mix the yogurt, harissa paste, cumin, minced garlic and olive oil together to form a thick dip. Keep chilled until you are ready to serve.

FRUIT & VEGETABLES

Almond tahini, 3 ways

Sometimes the sauce makes the dish, and when you find a great one, it is worth having different preparations for the different seasons. We are evoking the spirit of tahini (one of our favourite sauces) with this, but making it with almonds in their skins, which brings a great nuttiness. We serve this at Honey & Smoke with peaches in summer, pears in autumn and sweet potatoes in winter. Spring is reserved for green vegetables and they don't really work with this almond tahini, so we make a special, luxurious pistachio version instead to drizzle over grilled spring greens, dressed with lots of lime juice.

100 g / 3½ oz whole raw almonds, skins on.

100 g / 3½ oz boiling water

1 small clove of garlic, peeled

4 tbsp light vegetable oil (e.g. sunflower or rapeseed)

½ tsp flaky sea salt (plus more to taste)

1 tbsp sherry vinegar (or use red wine vinegar)

80 ml / 2¾ fl oz very cold water

Pour the boiling water over the almonds and set aside while they cool, for about 20–30 minutes. Drain, discard the water, and place the nuts in a food processor. Blitz to a very fine crumb, then add the garlic clove and continue blitzing as you pour in the vegetable oil. Pulse in the sprinkling of sea salt and the vinegar, and finally add the cold water, continuing to mix until everything is well-combined. Taste, and adjust the seasoning as necessary. It may seem a little runny now but the sauce will thicken as it settles. You may even need to add a touch more water and salt to loosen it just before serving.

Sweet potatoes baked in the embers, with almond tahini and smoked almonds

Serves 4

4 sweet potatoes, each about 300 g/ 10½ oz

flaky sea salt

1 portion of almond tahini (see left)

100 g / 3½ oz smoked almonds, chopped

1–2 tbsp date molasses (or honey)

Wash the skin of the sweet potatoes really well and wrap each one in aluminium foil so that it is fully covered. Place the foil parcels directly in the embers of your BBQ or fireplace (if you have one). They will take about 45–60 minutes to bake and soften, depending on their size, and it is worth turning them over every 10–15 minutes so that they cook evenly.

You can tell they are ready when the tip of a knife or a skewer can easily penetrate the whole way through. Pull the hot packages out of the embers and leave to cool for a few minutes until you can easily unwrap them.

When you are ready to serve, slit the still-warm sweet potatoes along their tops and push the sides out to reveal the soft inner flesh. Sprinkle with sea salt, spoon in a couple of dollops of almond tahini, top with the chopped smoked almonds and drizzle generously with date molasses before serving.

To cook without a BBQ

Sprinkle a thin layer of salt in a roasting tin, place the sweet potatoes on top (no need to wrap them in foil) and pop in the oven at 220°C/200°C fan/gas mark 7 for 40–45 minutes until soft.

Roasted pear with honey, almond tahini and rocket

Serves 4

4 large pears

3 tbsp extra virgin olive oil

2 tbsp red wine vinegar

2 tbsp honey

½ tsp Aleppo chilli flakes

flaky sea salt

freshly ground black pepper

100 g / 3½ oz wild rocket leaves

1 small bunch of coriander, leaves picked (about 30 g / 1 oz)

1 portion of almond tahini (see left)

Quarter and core the pears, place in a bowl and pour in the olive oil. Mix well to coat then remove the quarters (keep the oily bowl for the dressing) and place cut-side down on a medium-hot BBQ. Grill for about 1 minute on each side or until nice black griddle marks have formed.

Add the vinegar, honey, chilli flakes, and some salt and pepper to the oil you used to coat the pears, and stir it a little. As you lift the pear pieces off the grill, drop them into the dressing that has formed in the bowl. Mix well and set aside to marinate for 15–20 minutes.

Place the rocket and coriander leaves on a large serving platter. Top with the pears and all their juices, dollop with large spoonfuls of the almond tahini and serve immediately.

To cook without a BBQ

Use a lightly oiled, preheated griddle pan on your stove top and cook just as you would on the fire.

Grilled peaches with almond tahini and charred endive

Serves 4

4 endives

4 large, slightly firm peaches

3 tbsp olive oil to brush, and a little extra to drizzle

flaky sea salt

freshly ground black pepper

juice of ½ lemon

1 portion of almond tahini (see page 62)

1 handful of fresh mint leaves

Halve the endives and peaches, removing the stones from the peaches, then brush all the cut surfaces with olive oil. Place the endives and peaches cut-side down on a clean BBQ rack. Grill for about 3–4 minutes or until nice black griddle-marks have formed. Remove to a plate, season with salt and pepper, and drizzle the lemon juice all over. Spread two spoonfuls of almond tahini on each plate and top with two halves of charred endive and two halves of grilled peach. Add a sprinkling of fresh mint leaves and a drizzle of oil, then serve.

To cook without a BBQ

Use a lightly oiled, preheated griddle pan on your stove top and cook just as you would on the fire.

FRUIT & VEGETABLES

Haifa, Israel: Bonfire Night

Growing up in Israel, life felt like a succession of festivals, memorial days, high days and holidays, with a smattering of ordinary weekdays in between, keeping the year together. The calendar is full to the brim with holidays – some with their origins in religion or tradition, some ordinary state holidays – each with their own stories and customs, and obviously (most importantly) their own particular food.

Hanukkah for example, the festival of light, comes with the rains and shorter days of wintertime. It celebrates a heroic win over the Grecian army in the second century BC and the miracle of light, when one small bottle provided enough oil to light the holy flames in the temple for a whole week. Every night for eight days families gather around, lighting candles, singing songs and eating fried food: potato fritters, sweet and savoury doughnuts... by the end of the holiday everyone is that bit plumper, padding for the cold days ahead perhaps.

No less devastating to the waistline is the festival of Pentecost, *Shavuot*, which for some reason focuses on rich dairy and egg dishes – basically a whole weekend dedicated to the preparation and consumption of cheesecake, when both the cooking and the eating can become competitive activities.

On top of the regular New Year celebrations, there is also a New Year for the trees. Homes are decorated with branches of almond blossom, tables are laden with bowls of dried fruits and nuts, and children are taken to plant a tree.

During Passover you avoid bread for a fortnight and eat dry crackers instead. The trade-off for this is a magnificent spring feast of lamb and wine, and plenty of gifts for the kids.

Growing up, holidays were generally big family affairs, but bonfire night was just for us kids. In the weeks running up to the big event, alliances would be formed, broken and formed again. It involved no small amount of advanced planning to ensure that you and your group would have the best bonfire. Firewood needed to be obtained, and there were important things to be decided, in particular the three key elements for a good bonfire night: the Spot, the Stash and the Wheels. The Spot was where you would hold your bonfire; you needed to be there early to claim the best one. The Stash was where you kept your firewood until needed; it had to be well-hidden and protected, as the streets were full of marauding kids who would not hesitate to make your stash their own. The Wheels were crucial to the whole operation – how else would you get large amounts of wood from the source to the stash, and from there to the spot? Old baby buggies would be re-purposed, skateboards and bikes re-jigged to become wagons, and if you managed to get your hands on a supermarket trolley, then you'd hit the jackpot.

On the night itself the entire country smelt of smoke and everywhere you looked – on beaches, in fields, in fact in any open space – you would see the glow of bonfires and the shadows of people around them. What would we do? Just sit by the fire together. That's it; that was enough. Around every fire the same simple but extremely delicious food would be eaten – potatoes and onions wrapped in foil and threaded onto a metal wire so they could easily be pulled out of the embers. They looked like big, chunky necklaces of silver beads. The only skill required was knowing where to place the foil parcels (they have to cook on lively embers, since flaming wood will burn them and ash won't cook them). Then you simply poked a stick into a spud to check that it was ready. If the flesh gave easily, you would pull the entire string out of the fire and open the charred parcels as soon as you could handle them, the once-shiny foil baubles now indistinguishable from lumps of charcoal, revealing inside the smoky, tender flesh of potato and the soft, sweet, melting petals of onions seasoned with smoke. Nothing else was needed, not even salt.

This is not the only time of the year that this simple delicacy is eaten. Whenever a few people gather around a fire, some potatoes will be thrown in, but every child in Israel knows the flavour of bonfire night potatoes.

Baked potatoes with charred spring onion sour cream

Makes 4 filled potatoes, enough for 4 people (or 2 greedy ones)

As kids, while camping on youth movement trips, we would bake potatoes on the bonfire, threading them on a wire with a loop at one end to stick up from the embers, so that we could pull the cooked spuds out easily. We didn't wrap them as we do here, so the skins would be blackened and charred. As soon as we could touch them, we would use the charcoal to draw lines on our faces, pretending we were warriors. Then we would crack the potatoes open to reveal the steaming hot, light yellow flesh, eating with our hands. Without any dressing, or even any salt, they still tasted heavenly.

4 baking potatoes, each about 250 g / 9 oz

flaky sea salt, to taste

For the sour cream dressing

8–10 spring onions (a small bunch)

300 g / 10 ½ oz sour cream

1 large clove of garlic, peeled and minced

3 tbsp olive oil

½ tsp flaky sea salt

a good twist of black pepper

zest and juice of half a lemon

Wrap the potatoes individually in aluminium foil and place in the embers of the fire. Leave to cook until a knife or skewer goes in easily, about 40–45 minutes, turning them a couple of times while they bake.

In the meantime, char half the spring onions on the grill for about 2–3 minutes on each side until they have a great char. Remove from the heat and chop finely.

Finely slice the green sections of the uncooked spring onions and set aside to use as a garnish. Cut the remaining white sections into small pieces and stir into the sour cream along with the charred spring onion and all the other ingredients.

Once the potatoes are cooked, remove from the fire to cool and, as soon as you can handle them, peel away the aluminium foil. Cut each potato down the middle, sprinkle with some flaky sea salt and fill with the sour cream. Garnish with the finely sliced green spring onion before serving.

Any leftovers make a really great potato salad – simply remove the outer skins of the potatoes (or leave them on if you like a rustic salad), dice and mix with any leftover sour cream.

To cook without a BBQ

Sprinkle a thin layer of salt in a roasting tin, place the potatoes on top (no need to wrap them in foil) and pop in the oven at 220°C/200°C fan/gas mark 7 for 40–45 minutes until soft. Use a griddle pan to char the spring onions in a little olive oil.

Whole baked red onions with sage, honey and walnut dressing

Serves 6–8 as a starter or side salad

4 large red onions, skin on

olive oil for brushing

flaky sea salt, to finish

For the dressing

80 g / 2¾ oz walnuts

10 sage leaves, rolled up and cut into really thin strips

1 tbsp honey

2 tbsp white wine vinegar

2 tbsp boiling water

1 tsp mild chilli flakes

½ tsp salt

a little freshly ground black pepper

3 tbsp olive oil

a few sprigs of mint, leaves picked (about 15 g/ ½ oz)

Halve the red onions through the core, keeping the skin on. Brush the cut faces with oil and place cut-side down on a hot grill. Roast for about 12 minutes till the cut surface is black and charred, then flip skin-side down and leave to cook for a further 5 minutes. Remove to a plate to chill till they are cool enough to handle.

Make the dressing while you wait. Roast the walnuts over the fire for about 8 minutes in an old sieve or dry frying pan, stirring occasionally. Slightly crush them and mix with all the other dressing ingredients apart from the mint leaves.

Break the cooled onion halves into petals, discarding the outer skins. Set the petals with their charred rims upwards on a large serving plate. Just before serving, thinly shred the mint leaves and mix into the dressing. Drizzle all over the onion petals and sprinkle with a little sea salt to finish.

To cook without a BBQ

Use a lightly oiled, preheated griddle pan on your stove top and cook just as you would on the fire, but beware, your house will get pretty smoky!

Roasted celeriac with chive sour cream and *urfa* butter

Serves 4 as a starter or side

2 large heads of celeriac

2 tbsp olive oil

flaky sea salt

freshly ground black pepper

juice of 1 lemon

For the chive sour cream

150 g / 5¼ oz sour cream

50 g / 1¾ oz full fat Greek-style yogurt

2 large bunches of chives (about 60 g / 2¼ oz), finely chopped

2 tbsp olive oil

a pinch of freshly ground black pepper

For the *urfa* butter

50 g / 1¾ oz salted butter

1 tbsp *urfa* chilli flakes

Cut away the celeriac outer skin using a sharp knife. Wash well to get rid of any sand or dirt, then halve. Place each halved head on its own sheet of baking paper, drizzle with the olive oil and sprinkle with salt and pepper. Wrap the halved celeriac first in its baking paper and then in a sheet of aluminium foil. Place the four parcels very close to the fire, or even in the low embers, and cook slowly for about 25–30 minutes, turning occasionally, until a knife or skewer penetrates easily.

While the celeriac are cooking, make the chive sour cream by mixing all the ingredients together.

Carefully remove the parcels from the fire and, as soon as you can handle them, peel off the foil and paper. Cut the celeriac in thick slices, drizzle with the lemon juice and sprinkle with a little more salt.

Melt the butter in a little pan and let it start to bubble and foam, then remove from the heat, add the chilli and mix well to combine. Spoon the chive sour cream onto a plate, top with the celeriac slices and drizzle the *urfa* butter all over.

To cook without a BBQ

Sprinkle a thin layer of salt in a roasting tin, place the whole, unpeeled and unwrapped celeriac heads on top and pop in the oven at 220°C/200°C fan/gas mark 7 for 50–55 minutes until soft. Once baked, take them out of the tin and allow to cool, then peel away the skin so you are left with the soft flesh.

Turkey: Driving to Adana

In this part of southern Turkey you get a feeling of plenty, of a land so rich and generous that it almost bursts with goodness. It feels as if every bit of soil, left to its own devices, would sprout something good to eat. The earth is dark red, like blood or flesh; the air is humid along the banks of the mighty Seyhan River; and it is hot. Walking here, even in the colder months, you feel as if you're in a polytunnel. The good earth, the heat, the humidity – these are the conditions that polytunnels are designed to emulate, because this is what makes things grow. Grow fast, grow sweet and flavourful, grow big, grow delicious. You can see from the road how plump the sheep are on the verdant hilltops, flopping their fatty tails. Orchard trees bend under the weight of their fruit. Beautiful, colourful fields seem to explode, their produce overflowing into stalls at the side of the road, little huts full of rich abundance from the land nearby, tables bowed from the weight of pumpkins and squashes tanned to bright orange. The courgettes, squashes and marrows smell like honey, and the figs, big as the fists of the man selling them, are as sweet as a smile.

Punctuating the driveway-like road are signs saying Stop! Eat me! in carrot orange, strawberry red, or radish pink and green. A plume of smoke by a stall signals us to stop – something is cooking. There are piles of apples mottled red and green, bright pumpkins, shiny chestnuts. An older lady beaming a toothless smile sits next to a low fire which is barely burning and smells fragrant with fruitwood. On the fire is a crooked little pan of chestnuts, a teapot brewing and a whole pumpkin that she turns every so often. We can't speak her language and she cannot speak ours, but for the most part we communicate very well. We point at the chestnuts and get a cone of them, roasted and piping hot; we point to the tea and she pours cups for us; but when we point at the pumpkin, she does not understand – what do we want with her pumpkin? She points to the stalls where the pumpkins are laid out for sale, clearly asking, "Do you want one?" We shake our heads; no, we want to try yours! No, she insists. We don't know why. Maybe she was saving it for later, or maybe it wasn't yet cooked. We paid for our tea and chestnuts, got back into our car and continued driving to Adana.

We didn't get to taste fire-roasted pumpkin till we got back to London and fired up our own grill; now we have an idea why the lady didn't want to share.

Grilled pumpkins, apples and chestnuts

Serves 4 as a starter or 6 as a side

1 small pumpkin or 2 small
onion squash

2 Golden Delicious or Pink
Lady apples

2 tbsp olive oil

1 tsp sea salt

½ tsp freshly ground black pepper

12 chestnuts

1 head of red radicchio or red endive

For the dressing

juice of 1 orange

2 tbsp cider vinegar

5 cm / 2 inch piece of fresh ginger,
peeled and grated

2 tbsp dried barberries (or you can use
dried currants)

1 tbsp honey

2 tbsp olive oil

Mix all the dressing ingredients together
and set aside until you are ready to serve.
If you can, make it at least one hour in
advance of serving, for the best flavour.

Cut the pumpkin into thick slices or
wedges (no need to peel), remove the
seeds and place on a baking tray. Slice
the apples into 2–3 cm / ¾–1¼ inch
thick rounds (cut through the core) and
add to the tray. Drizzle with the olive oil
and season with the sea salt and pepper.
Remove from the tray and place the
pumpkin and apple slices on a hot grill
to char for about 3–4 minutes on each
side, then return them to the oily tray.

Slit the chestnuts carefully with a sharp
knife so they don't explode and place in
a mesh tray or colander over the fire to
roast. Shake the tray / colander every
30 seconds or so, till the skins crisp and
start to open – about 12–14 minutes.

Break the radicchio into separate
leaves, place on a large platter and top
with the slices of grilled pumpkin and
apple. Peel the chestnuts and break them
up, scattering the pieces all over the
salad, then dress generously and serve.

To cook without a BBQ

Roast the oiled, seasoned pumpkin in a
hot oven at 220°C/200°C fan/gas mark 7
for about 20 minutes, then transfer to a
griddle pan over a medium-high heat to
char for 3–4 minutes each side. Griddle
the oiled and seasoned apples on both
sides for the same length of time. Roast
the chestnuts in the oven for about
10 minutes until the skins start to open,
but don't forget to score them first.

FRUIT & VEGETABLES

Figs with manouri cheese and pomegranate dressing

Makes 4 skewers

This isn't a complex recipe, but it showcases two lovely ingredients in the best way possible. We have a big fig tree by our house and use the leaves to wrap the cheese, which imparts a subtle, special flavour. Try it if you can. If you are struggling to source pomegranate molasses, mix a tablespoon of honey with a teaspoon of red wine vinegar and use this instead.

4 large, plump figs, halved

2 thick slices of manouri cheese (or you can use haloumi), cut into quarters

flaky sea salt

coarsely ground black pepper

For the pomegranate dressing

2 sprigs of rosemary, leaves picked

2 sprigs of thyme, leaves picked

1 green chilli, sliced as thinly as you can

strips of peel from 1 lemon (use a strip zester or grater)

2 tbsp pomegranate molasses

4 tbsp olive oil

5 sprigs of mint, leaves picked and coarsely chopped

1 handful of pomegranate seeds

Make the dressing first, as the figs and cheese only take a few minutes to char. Chop the rosemary and thyme together as finely as you can, then mix in the sliced chilli, lemon peel strips, pomegranate molasses and two tablespoons of the olive oil. Just before serving stir in the roughly chopped mint and a handful of pomegranate seeds.

Thread two fig halves alternately with two pieces of cheese on each skewer. Brush the figs and cheese all over with the remaining olive oil and place on a very hot BBQ to colour and sear. This will only take 3–4 minutes. Transfer to a serving plate, sprinkle with salt and pepper, top with the dressing and serve straight away for the best flavour.

To cook without a BBQ

Use a lightly oiled, preheated griddle pan on your stove top and cook just as you would on the fire, though it may be easier to do this without the skewers.

Spiced courgettes with goats' yogurt and grapes

A light lunch for 2–3 or a great starter for 6

12 baby green courgettes

2 garlic cloves, peeled and crushed

3 tbsp olive oil

flaky sea salt

freshly ground black pepper

juice of 1 lemon

Spices

1 tsp ground cumin

1 tsp ground coriander

a pinch of freshly ground black pepper

a pinch of chilli flakes or cayenne pepper

½ tsp ground ginger

½ tsp ground cinnamon

½ tsp flaky sea salt

To serve

150 g / 5¼ oz black seedless grapes, halved

40 g / 1½ oz pine nuts, lightly roasted

1 small bunch of mint, leaves picked

100 g / 3½ oz goats' yogurt

Halve the courgettes lengthways and use a small knife to score the flesh with a criss-cross pattern (make sure not to go through to the skin). Set on a tray. Mix the crushed garlic with the olive oil and brush some of this mixture generously over the cut surfaces, then season with salt and black pepper. Place the courgettes cut-side down directly on the grill rack to colour for 3–4 minutes, then flip them over so that they are cut-side up. Mix all the spices into the remaining garlic oil to form a thick paste and brush it over the cut surfaces of each courgette, making sure it gets into the scored grooves. Leave to cook for another 3–4 minutes, then remove from the grill onto a serving plate.

Spoon over any remaining garlic-oil-paste and drizzle with the lemon juice. Top with the grapes, pine nuts, mint leaves and small dollops of the yogurt, and serve.

To cook without a BBQ

Use a lightly oiled, preheated griddle pan on your stove top and cook just as you would on the fire.

Fish & Seafood

The Eastern Mediterranean has been sadly over-fished for many years. While there are now laws, quotas and specific months during the breeding season when fishing is entirely prohibited – all rules designed to protect fishing stocks, – this doesn't always work in practice, as much of the fishing is done from small boats which zip in and out of harbours along the coast, unnoticed by the authorities. It's wise to be a little picky and ask the right questions to make sure the fish you are buying are actually sustainably caught and local. The best fish for the BBQ are oily ones – sardines, anchovy, salmon, bonito (also known as Spanish mackerel or palamida) and local blue fin tuna – as they stay moist and work well with the smoky flavour.

If you can, buy whole fish in the market where you may be choosing from that morning's catch, and where you can check for signs of freshness:

- a clean sea-water smell – fresh fish never smells fishy
- bright, clear eyes – sunken or dried eyes are a sign that the fish has been sitting around for a long time
- bright red gills – not a dull maroon
- flesh which resists and bounces back when pressed – it shouldn't sink or stay dented

Of course, your local fishmonger or the fisherman on the quayside may not appreciate you poking at their display, but hopefully you trust your fishmonger, and as for the fisherman, if you are lucky you will have seen him unload the catch straight from the boat. One thing is for sure, it doesn't hurt to know what to look out for.

When buying cuts of tuna and salmon you obviously won't be able to check the eyes or gills, but do still try to get a sniff and, if you can, press to check the firmness of the flesh. It is harder to judge the freshness of a cut, but the good news is that tuna and salmon last well – indeed modern fish butchery techniques actually involve aging certain fish like tuna and swordfish in a manner similar to aging meat. Fillets also dry out more quickly on the grill than whole fish do, so opt for nice thick pieces and serve them slightly pink for best results.

That's all there is to it – fish cooks fantastically over fire and is quick, easy and healthy. Just watch out for those pesky bones.

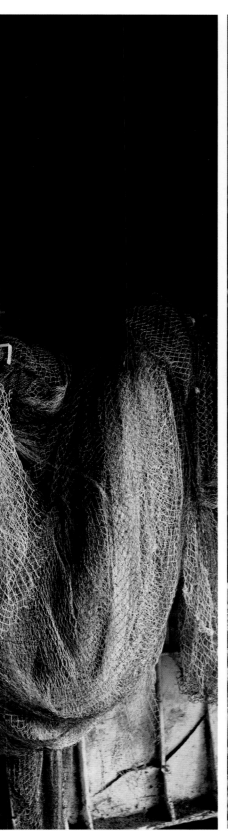

Thessaloniki, Greece: Treasure hunt

Some cities keep to themselves, holding the visitor at arm's length, so that you feel as if you are looking in from the outside, but not Thessaloniki. She's a friendly, welcoming hostess. For centuries a port town, she is used to visitors coming and going, and she seems to enjoy travellers passing through. Nestled in a sparkling bay on the Aegean Sea, Greece's second city sees herself as second to none.

Even in winter, life here takes place outdoors. People meet up on the tree-lined avenues that spill down to the sea. Tables and chairs cover the pavements outside the bustling restaurants, cafés and bars, where groups of Thessalonians set the world to rights, or just take in the day. The big and small dramas of city life play out on the generous balconies that adorn every building in town: you can hear neighbours' conversations being shouted between blocks, and on warm nights some people will drag the TV onto the balcony and spend the evening there, munching on salt-roasted seeds of watermelon and pumpkin. We saw a block of flats by the outdoor cinema, balconies full of freeloaders craning their necks to catch the show.

Walking into a local coffee shop we struck up a conversation with an old sailor who insisted we go to a nearby bakery which makes 'the best *koulouri* in town'. These, we learned, are bread rings, usually encrusted in sesame; a bit like a Turkish *simit* or a Jerusalem bagel, but firmer and crunchier, and so

much more than merely a bakery item in Thessaloniki – our sailor friend told us they are revered as the taste of the town. However, it seems that bakeries in this city are like football clubs: within minutes the whole café crowd was up in arms, each group swearing that their favourite bakery made the best *koulouri*. But, like choosing a football club, you usually go with the first one you know, so we went with our old sailor's recommendation and set off to the bakery up the road, following the scent of freshly-baked bread. The two friendly bakers there were surrounded with twisted golden rings of dough, fresh out of the oven, bejewelled in sesame seeds, in salt, in poppy seeds, in chopped walnuts, and all hanging from wooden pegs on the wall. We went for the classic, obviously, the rich layer of sesame seeds crackling as we bit into the crunchy bread. Suddenly we could see why it would make the locals so emotional.

Chatting with the bakers, they suggested that we visit Serraikon, a bakery founded in the 1950s and famous for its *bougatsa*. We had never heard of *bougatsa*, but by now we felt we were on a culinary treasure hunt, so we followed their directions towards the market.

We found Serraikon at the entrance to the old market, just as promised. The shop is not much more than a hole in the wall, with a small window and a few tables scattered around outside. The *bougatsa* is laid on trays by the window

and pieces are sliced for you with a small crescent knife. The crunchy filo makes little cracking sounds as it is cut, the knife carving through layers of thin, crisp pastry encasing a hot semolina pudding, flavoured with vanilla and perhaps orange blossom as well – we couldn't quite tell – topped with a good dusting of icing sugar and cinnamon which blows into your nose and powders your chin as you eat. Bliss!

Walking around a food market on holiday abroad is both heaven and hell for a keen cook. You are so tempted by all the beautiful produce – you know just how good those plump chickens would taste, those field-fresh green beans. You are curious about a particular vegetable you've never seen before, and about that delicious-smelling herb. You want to buy it all, but what can you do with it? Take it to your hotel room or your weekend rental flat? Pack it in your suitcase for the long flight home?

We walked around that market like kids in a candy shop, eyeing up fresh Mediterranean fish arranged on blocks of ice, gleaming silver and red, and smelling of sea spray; a huge variety of olives and olive oil; then the aisle of meats, with various unknown cuts hanging from hooks. Was that a goat? A sheep? Part of a cow? We are chefs and still we couldn't tell.

We have developed the habit of following older people in these local markets as they always seem to know where the good stuff is.

In Sicily we once stalked a *nonna* buying artichokes who led us to a truck in a parking lot that was selling fried fish, some of the best we have ever had. Here, we soon found ourselves following a distinguished-looking gentleman who was greeted by everyone around. He was checking out the day's catch, choosing only the finest that each stall had to offer. The tiny octopus here looked good; he picked a few up in his hand and brought them to his nose – they clearly smelled good too – as, with a nod of the head, he signalled to the stallholder to pack them for him, all of them. At another stall he poked his finger into the bright red gills of some big bonito, and again he took them all. Next he turned his attention to big, juicy prawns. This man was buying everything that we wanted to eat; we had a hunch that he was a good man to make friends with. In our minds he was either hosting a big fishy dinner party to which we would try to wangle an invitation, or he ran a restaurant, where those carefully chosen fish could be cooked for us. Either way we needed to make our move, so we said hi. He didn't have much English but gave a smile; a promising start. We pointed at the bonito with a thumbs-up: Nice fish you have there. He splayed the fingers of one hand, placed the other hand on top and made a hissing sound – the splayed fingers were the grill, the other hand the fish; he was going to grill them – then kissed two fingers: It's going to be good. We pointed at ourselves, then at

our mouths; a crude but very effective way of saying, We want in! We want your beautiful grilled bonito, and from his suit pocket he pulled a card. The stallholder watching this theatre piped up "Best fish restaurant in town!". The gentleman beamed at him, and we took the card, hoping that dinner would be every bit as good as the show we had just witnessed.

The unofficial motto of this town is *chalara*, which roughly translates as 'chill'. We learned this in another café, having our second coffee of the day. We struck up a conversation with a young, local hipster girl who had lived in London for a while. She also taught us the basics of the Greek alphabet and how to write our names in it. As we sat together in the mid-morning sun, she recommended a nice beach just out of town. Later that day we headed there to relax for a while by the sea, but when we arrived we accidentally burrowed our car into the flat white sands, mistaking them for a stable and secure road. As we sank deeper in the sand, a couple in a jeep stopped and, with the most gracious of airs, simply pulled out a rope, attached it to their jeep and towed us out, as if this was something which happened every day. They invited us to join their sunset picnic, and we wished we could have stayed, got to know them, but we had to run. We had a date with a lovely old gentleman and some grilled bonito, and hopefully, those tiny octopods as well.

Octopus with paprika aïoli

Every octopus has 8 legs – allow 2 per person

Grilled octopus is not purely a BBQ dish, as it needs slow braising before it ever reaches the fire, but it is ideal for an outdoor party. Braise and marinate it in advance, then keep it chilled until needed. When you're ready to serve, a quick turn on a hot grill will produce perfect results. We prefer to use frozen ones, rather than fresh, and thaw them overnight in the sink, as they have a better texture once cooked.

1 large octopus (defrosted)

For the braising liquor

1 plum tomato, quartered

1 red onion, quartered

1 tsp whole cumin seeds

1 tsp whole black peppercorns

4 garlic cloves, halved

1 chilli, halved lengthways

2 bay leaves

a few sprigs of sage

4 tbsp red wine (or use white, if there's some open, or 2 tbsp brandy)

Place the octopus in a large pot (ideally heavy-bottomed with a fitted lid) with all the braising ingredients and cover. Place the pot on a hot grill or in the oven at 220°C/200°C fan/gas mark 6 for 1 hour. Open the pot carefully and use a pair of tongs or a large spoon to turn the octopus over. Re-cover the pot and return to the heat for another 20–30 minutes until the octopus is cooked – a small knife should easily pierce the thickest part, just by the head, and the flesh should have a slightly spongy texture. If there is too much resistance or the octopus feels rubbery, cook for a further 10–15 minutes. Allow to cool in the cooking liquid.

Drain the octopus in a colander (you can discard the cooking liquid or boil potatoes in it, if you like the flavour), then lay it on a chopping board and cut the head (the round cap) away from the star-shaped body and legs. Halve the head lengthways, clean it inside and out, and set in a bowl. Slice the body in half and remove the tough ball in the middle. Cut the legs away from the body and, if they are very long, chop them in half. Place in the bowl with the halved head.

For the marinade

1 clove of garlic, thinly sliced

8 sage leaves, roughly chopped

1 tsp smoked paprika

a sprinkle of chilli flakes

3 tbsp olive oil

Add all the marinade ingredients to the octopus pieces in the bowl and mix well. Store in the fridge for up to 48 hours, until you are ready to grill.

For the paprika aïoli

1 egg yolk

1 small clove of garlic, minced

½ tsp smoked paprika

½ tsp sweet paprika

a pinch of salt, plus more to taste

2 tsp rice vinegar (or light white wine vinegar)

100–120 ml / 3½–4¼ fl oz vegetable oil

juice of ½ lemon

Whisk the egg yolk, garlic, paprikas, salt and vinegar together (by hand or in a food processor) until well-combined. Continue to whisk as you drizzle the oil in a slow, steady stream, and keep whisking while the mixture thickens and forms an emulsion. Once all the oil has been incorporated and the aïoli has a nice creamy consistency, whisk in the lemon juice a little at a time, enough to suit your taste buds. Adjust the seasoning as necessary, then store in the fridge until needed.

When you are ready to cook, set the octopus pieces on a hot grill, rotating them every 2–3 minutes until they are lightly charred all over. Serve with the paprika aïoli.

To cook without a BBQ

Use a lightly oiled, preheated griddle pan on your stove and cook just as you would on the fire.

Sardines grilled in vine leaves

We usually allow 2 sardines per person, but you may need to adjust this depending on the size of the fish

Preserved or pickled vine leaves are used extensively around the Eastern Mediterranean, usually to wrap flavoured rice, and each country has its own version. They also work well as a layer of seasoning and protection between a fire and a delicate piece of fish (or cheese), as here. You can buy a huge jar and work your way through it slowly, as long as you retain the brine, or buy a small vacuum pack of 20 or so leaves, sufficient for this recipe. If you are lucky enough to have a grape vine growing in your garden, simply blanch some of the larger leaves in plenty of salty water before using.

8–16 vine leaves (depending on their size), preserved in brine

1 lemon, cut into 8 thin slices

4 sprigs of thyme

4 sardines (each about 150 g / 5¼ oz), gutted and scaled

1 garlic clove, peeled and thinly sliced

olive oil for drizzling

freshly ground black pepper

Lay 2–4 vine leaves on the table with a slight overlap between them to create a continuous sheet of leaves large enough to wrap a sardine easily. Place a slice of lemon and a sprig of thyme in the centre of the sheet, and top with a sardine. Place a slice of lemon in the belly cavity along with a couple of slices of garlic. Drizzle the fish with olive oil, add a twist of black pepper, and fold the leaves around the fish like an envelope. Repeat with the other three. Grill the fish parcels on a hot BBQ for 4–5 minutes until the leaves start to burn slightly, then carefully flip them over and cook the other side. Serve immediately.

To cook without a BBQ

Place the fish on a rack on top of a roasting tin in a very hot oven (240°C/220°C fan/gas mark 9) and cook for 5 minutes on each side.

Grilled squid and summer vegetables

Dinner for 4 or a starter for 6–8

Squid is holiday food for us: calamari in a Greek taverna, freshly-caught and fried in a crisp coating, meltingly soft inside; or hot off the grill, the edges burnt to crunchy, smoky-sweet perfection. That particular saline taste works really well with a garlicky dipping sauce and a fresh sea breeze. Alternatively, serve it as we do here, with a bunch of vegetables all roasted together on the grill.

4 large squid (or 8 small), cleaned and dried

5 baby courgettes, halved lengthways (or 2 large courgettes, thickly sliced)

1 lemon, cut into 6 wedges

a drizzle of olive oil

1 tsp dried oregano

flaky sea salt

freshly ground black pepper

20 cherry tomatoes (on the vine is best, if possible)

For the marinade

strips of peel from 1 lemon (use a peeler)

2 red chillies, halved, deseeded and thinly sliced

juice of 1 lemon

4–5 sprigs of thyme, leaves picked and chopped

2 tbsp olive oil

a pinch of flaky sea salt

a pinch of freshly ground black pepper

Slit each squid lengthways along the natural seam lines, where the quill was attached, to create two large triangles. Use a sharp knife to hatch little crisscross cuts all over the inner surface of the squid (just score the flesh; don't cut through). Set in a large bowl.

Combine the marinade ingredients. Mix half into the squid and keep the rest for later. Leave to marinate in the fridge for at least 20 minutes, but no longer than a couple of hours. Drizzle the courgettes and lemon with olive oil. Make sure your BBQ is really hot before placing the lemon wedges cut-side down on the grill. Flip them over after 3–4 minutes to colour the other cut surface, then remove to a platter. Place the courgettes cut-side down on the grill and allow to really char and get clear griddle marks, about 4–5 minutes, then flip and cook the other side for 3–4 minutes too. Remove to the same platter as the lemons. Season the grilled courgettes with the oregano and sprinkle with salt and pepper. Put the cherry tomatoes on the grill to colour all over: you can cook them in a little sieve over the fire to stop them rolling around or place them straight on the BBQ, if they are still on the vine. Once cooked, add to the other vegetables. Place the squid flat on the BBQ, scored-side down, and sprinkle with salt and pepper. They will quickly curl up. Flip to the other side for a minute, before removing and adding to the grilled vegetables. Transfer everything to a serving platter, drizzle with the remaining marinade and serve.

To cook without a BBQ

Use a lightly oiled, preheated griddle pan on your stove and cook just as you would on the fire.

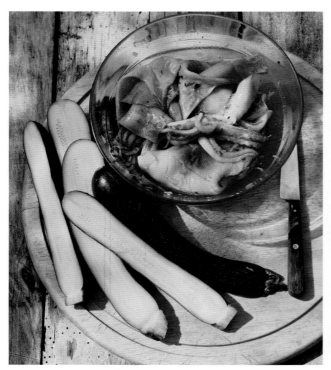

Alexandria, Egypt:
Three taxis

We arrived in Alexandria with a comprehensive list of 'must-try' restaurants given to us by Mustafa, a kindly cabby in whose car we spent over an hour navigating the mad traffic of Cairo. Originally from Alexandria, he was keen to give us tips on how to get the most pleasure out of his beloved hometown, and we were equally keen to write them all down. We set great store by the culinary knowledge of cabbies and their easy familiarity with a town. Top of the list was Hosny, so that was our first destination, not far from the Montaza Palace gardens; a pleasant walk from our hotel to the top of the Corniche, the promenade that runs along the shore. They call this town *arouset el bahr*, the bride of the sea, and her husband certainly showers her with his gifts. The whole strip is lined with fishermen and little fishing boats, and the restaurants selling their catches stretch along the road, each displaying their produce arranged on ice outside so that you can check for yourself – which one has the best, the freshest.

Hosny has a display of fish at its entrance just like everywhere else, but it feels a little grander than the other restaurants, with its elegant foyer in a faded French style. It was early evening, but the place was already buzzing and everyone was welcome: big families sat together having an early dinner before the kids had to go to bed; there was an elderly couple treating themselves; and a man with his car keys and phone on the table, his wife tending to the kids

with manicured hands. Two musicians strolled from table to table, one strumming an *oud*, the other beating a *darbuka*. They played one of the much-loved songs of Egyptian singer and actress Umm Kulthum; her music could be heard everywhere in the city.

The room was run by three young men, their faces so alike we guessed they must be brothers, or at least cousins. One of them handed us menus and a little plastic basket filled with wet wipes, saying *Tualet!* He looked expectantly at us; we looked back enquiringly at him. He gestured at us to wipe our hands and repeated *Tualet!* We duly did as instructed, and with clean hands we followed him back to the foyer to choose our food.

We looked into the glass-fronted fridge at beautifully-arranged meat: a spiral of chops on one platter, a whirl of lamb's kidneys on another, as well as stacks of koftas on skewers, speckled green and white with parsley and fat visible through the caul wrapping, all displayed on a verdant bed of herbs. Our eyes strayed to the kitchen, clearly visible behind. There were chefs rolling kofta and trimming sweetbreads, and waiters bringing baskets of fish to be cooked on the roaring grill which spanned the length of an entire wall. The chefs were friendly and let us into the depths of their kitchen to inspect the grill and the laden shelves of meats. Eventually our waiter signalled for us to follow him back to the entrance, where we had yet to choose our fish from the

display: wild bream, with its distinctive yellow forehead, massive groupers, tiny clams, bright scarlet prawns as big as an outstretched hand, and everything as fresh as could be.

Of course, we wanted it all. The obligatory mezze was followed by a procession of grilled food, some of the best we've ever had. An unexpected platter of offal arrived – brain, kidneys, liver, testicles – all expertly cooked, fresh and delicious. This was followed by those big red prawns, that gilthead bream...

Replete, we sat back in our chairs as the musicians came back for another circuit. The waiters cleared the tables, arranging the plates in tall stacks, the first layer in petal formation, the second layer weighing down the first and so on, creating tier after tier till they ended up with a huge towering flower. The two older men were trying to teach their little brother how to do it, and they simply laughed as he dropped all the plates on the floor.

We ended our meal with glasses of fresh mint tea and more of the inevitable wet wipes (*Tualet!*) and saw our cheeky waiter looking over his shoulder as he pocketed the tip we had left; he was not going to share it with his brothers.

The cab ride back to the hotel proved to be something we'd rather never repeat. Alexandria is served by a taxi fleet of boxy, late 1970s/early 1980s yellow and black Ladas, which look great in a jolly, retro manner.

FISH & SEAFODD

We thought it'd be a good idea to take one (for an authentic Alexandrian experience) but it really wasn't. The car reeked of decades of cigarette smoke and diesel fumes, there were no seatbelts or any real suspension, and we sank into the back seat and held on for dear life as loud music throbbed from the car radio and the ill-tempered driver continually blared his horn. We arrived back in our hotel 20 minutes later and a year older, throwing currency at the driver as he shouted something rude at us.

The next day we decided to go to another place on Mustafa's list, but this time we booked an Uber taxi. We thought it would be safer, such was our belief in western technology. Our driver was a friendly young guy and we told him where we wanted to go. When we asked if it was a nice restaurant, he shrugged a little and said it was okay. Very soon we saw that our driver was heading in completely the wrong direction, the little car icon on the Uber map steering further and further

away from the restaurant. Alarmed, we showed him our map, and he cheerfully explained that he was taking us to a much better restaurant – to Hosny. But, we protested, we had already eaten at Hosny the night before. "Good place, no? The best restaurant in Alexandria!" He did not understand our desire to go anywhere else, but we were adamant, and he reluctantly agreed to change course.

He dropped us next to a strip mall that looked rather derelict, but he pointed at it and said, "Go there." We threaded our way past shops that looked as if the owners had closed for lunch and never come back, a car showroom with no cars, and an escalator that led to a floor above that hadn't even been built – a stairway to nowhere. As everywhere in Egypt, there were gangs of street cats, and old men sitting on plastic chairs in shady corners. But then there was the distinct smell of grilling meats and a huge, humming extractor fan outlet; it was a restaurant, and obviously a working one. We had finally found it.

At the entrance were two big cages filled with green and grey parrots, and a big fish tank that had outdated Happy New Year banners hanging from side to side. Inside, the dining room was so huge it felt deserted even though there were quite a lot of people there. We were seated at a table that could easily have accommodated twenty, on banquettes that were way too low – the table top was almost at shoulder height. We felt like small children, even more so when the waiter brought us a thick mattress to use as a booster seat. We managed, somehow, to order, and ploughed through our meal, the usual fare: mezze, bread, grilled meat. It was decent enough but the whole experience was so surreal that we had to admit, our rogue Uber driver was right – we would have been better off at Hosny's, with a plate of those delicious scarlet prawns.

Prawns in honey and fresh coriander

Makes 4 skewers

Nothing compares to the flavour and colour of large Mediterranean prawns. They are hard to come by away from the Med, but well worth the search. Fast and furious cooking on an open flame gives them a great flavour. We keep the skins on while grilling so they don't dry out, but we carefully slit the back of the shell before marinating to remove the digestive tract and allow the flavours to penetrate through. Make sure to serve the skewers with a finger bowl alongside, as things will get messy.

8 large shell-on prawns

4 red chillies

For the marinade

1 large bunch of coriander, top part of the bunch (about 40 g / 1½ oz)

½ small bunch of mint, leaves picked (about 15 g / ½ oz)

1 large clove of garlic, peeled

1 green chilli, halved and seeds removed

1 tsp dried mint

zest of 1 lemon

½ tsp sea salt

a pinch of freshly ground black pepper

1 tbsp honey

3 tbsp olive oil

Place all the marinade ingredients apart from the honey and olive oil in a food processor, or, if you are feeling full of energy, use a pestle and mortar. Whizz or pound everything to a rough paste. Remove from the processor, if blitzing, and stir in the honey and oil by hand (the honey makes things too sticky if blitzed in the processor, and you don't want the oil to emulsify in the machine).

Slit the prawns down the back of their shells and use a knife tip to remove the digestive tract. Mix half the marinade in with the prawns and set in the fridge (along with the rest of the marinade in a separate bowl) for 20–60 minutes before cooking.

Thread each skewer with two prawns and one chilli, piercing the prawns from head to tail and sandwiching the chilli in between them.

Grill on a very high heat until the prawns turn a bright pink or for about 4 minutes on each side (the red Mediterranean prawns won't change colour so you'll need to time them). Remove to a serving plate, drizzle with the remaining marinade and make sure to provide plenty of napkins and a finger bowl.

To cook without a BBQ

Use a lightly oiled, preheated griddle pan on your stove and cook just as you would on the fire.

Grilled watermelon and prawns with feta and chilli

To serve 4 as a light lunch

Cooking the prawns with the shell on allows them to stay juicy and moist while taking on the great smoky flavour from the BBQ. If you use pre-peeled prawns they will only need a really fast flash on the grill, to avoid over-cooking.

12 large prawns or 16 smaller ones, whole and with shell on

half a small watermelon (or 2 thick slices of a large watermelon)

1 red chilli, sliced into rings

2 tbsp red wine vinegar

½ tsp salt

250 g / 9 oz sheeps' feta

1 small bunch of mint, leaves picked, half of them chopped, the rest left whole

3 tbsp olive oil, plus a little more for brushing on the watermelon

1 tsp roughly crushed black pepper

To prepare the prawns, use a sharp serrated knife to score a slit down the back shell of each one, cutting through the flesh to reveal the digestive string. Remove it with the tip of the knife. Put the cleaned prawns in a bowl in the fridge until you are ready to cook (once you start, you will only need 15 minutes to get this dish to the table). Cut the watermelon into eight large wedges, keeping the skin on. Mix the chilli slices with the vinegar and salt, and set aside while you build your BBQ to a high heat with lovely glowing embers.

Start by grilling the watermelon – simply brush the pieces with some olive oil and lay them flat on the hottest part of the grill for about 1–2 minutes each side. You want to form black grid marks on the flesh, as this will intensify the flavour and sweeten the fruit. Remove the melon to a side platter, then grill the prawns for 3 minutes on each side (2 minutes for smaller ones) or until they turn bright pink.

Add the prawns to the watermelon, crumble the feta over them, and scatter with the whole picked mint leaves. Just before serving, stir the olive oil, black pepper and chopped mint into the marinating chilli and drizzle all over the platter. Serve immediately with a finger bowl and another bowl for shells.

To cook without a BBQ

Use a lightly oiled, preheated griddle pan on your stove and cook just as you would on the fire.

FISH & SEAFOOD

Pilpel chuma – bream on the grill

Serves 2 but really easy to scale up (allow one fish per person)

2 large sea bream, about 600 g / 21 oz each

½ lemon, cut into thin slices

For the *pilpel chuma* marinade

5–6 garlic cloves, peeled and minced (about 30 g / 1 oz)

100 g / 3½ oz tomato purée

1 tsp chilli flakes

1 tsp smoked paprika

1 tsp sweet paprika

1 tsp ground cumin

½ tsp ground turmeric

2 tbsp olive oil

½ tsp salt

2 tbsp lemon juice

Start by cleaning, gutting and descaling the fish (or get your fishmonger to do it for you). Using a sharp knife, cut long thin slits along the whole fish, all the way down to the bone, about 1 cm / ½ inch apart.

Mix the *pilpel chuma* ingredients together to form a paste. Rub a third of the marinade all over the skin of the fish, including into the slits, and fill the bellies with the lemon slices.

Place the fish on a medium-hot grill and cook for 4 minutes on one side. Flip them over, brush the cooked side with another third of the marinade, and leave to grill for a further 4 minutes. Flip them again and brush the remaining marinade on the just-cooked side. Flip the fish back over for a final minute's grilling, then serve.

To cook without a BBQ

Place the fish on a rack on top of a roasting tin in a very hot oven (240°C/220°C fan/gas mark 9) and follow the method above for timings, turnings and bastings.

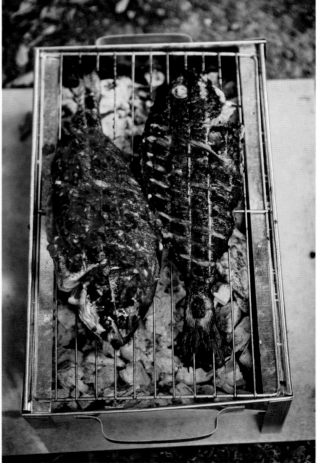

Tuna shish with *chermoula* and preserved lemons

Makes 4 skewers – allow 2 per person for a meal

Tuna is a very robust fish so it cooks beautifully on a BBQ, it retains flavour and moisture and the slight smokiness works well with the oiliness of the fish. The *chermoula* paste is a spicy lemony number that adds real zing – it will keep well in your fridge for a few days, so if there is any left over or you are inclined to double the amount you make, it will work well in a tinned tuna salad or in a sandwich with salted or cured beef. Serve the shish with baked potatoes for a hearty meal.

2 good, quality, thick tuna steaks (about 400 g / 14 oz in total)

a drizzle of olive oil, for brushing

flaky sea salt

freshly ground black pepper

juice of half a lemon

For the *chermoula*

2 preserved lemons, skin only (pulp and seeds removed)

1 clove of garlic

½ red chilli

1 bunch of coriander, top part only

½ bunch of parsley, leaves picked

freshly ground black pepper

½ tsp ground coriander

about 50 ml / 1¾ fl oz olive oil

We like to make this *chermoula* by hand, chopping everything until very fine, then mixing it with the oil in a small bowl. You could use a pestle and mortar instead to pound the ingredients, in which case add the oil at the end once everything else is well-combined.

Cut each tuna steak into four large cubes and thread two on each skewer. Brush well with olive oil, sprinkle with salt and pepper, and place on a very hot grill to cook and char nice lines. Turn the skewers after a minute and repeat twice more to char the tuna cubes for a minute on each side. We rather like the interior a little raw, but if you don't, simply cook for 30 seconds more on each side. Remove from the grill, douse with the lemon juice, then top with the *chermoula*.

To cook without a BBQ

Use a lightly oiled, preheated griddle pan on your stove and cook just as you would on the fire. Or you could simply use a non-stick frying pan.

Acre, Israel: Facing the sea

The old town of Akko (also known as Acre) is a terribly romantic place, conjuring up the atmosphere of any number of oriental stories, from *The Arabian Nights* to those of Lawrence of Arabia and Agatha Christie. It is a medieval fortified city, encircled by ancient walls of white stone, situated on a pretty bay with Haifa to the south and the border with Lebanon to the north. Inside the walls is a maze of ancient streets, opening up to squares and covered markets, arches and stairs and doorways, all in decorated stone. There's an Ottoman-era clock tower and four old *khan* (caravanserai). These colonnaded courtyards were used to house caravans of camels and their riders travelling along the trade and spice routes from Asia to Africa and Europe (Akko lies conveniently close to the points where these continents meet). There are mosques with their domes and minarets in bright green, resplendent against the blue of sea and sky. There are fine halls and crusader-built tunnels that lead underground from one side of the city to the other, and the remains of a small crusader-era port which was reserved for Italian maritime traders in the Pisan Quarter. Altogether it's a lively town, full of activity: battle-scarred cats roam the streets, unafraid of anyone; hawk-eyed matrons on balconies watch over young kids in the yard; rude boys race down the streets on bikes, pushing aside visitors with big cameras; young men loiter in the crumbling old inns with their horses and donkeys, smoking shisha or weed, pitting roosters against each other.

Akko is still a fishing town with a fishing town's rhythm. Most of the boats head out to sea from the small port before dawn, when it is still dark; some leave even earlier, in the dead of night, but they are all back by early morning with their catch. By then the town is in full swing. Bakery boys rush through the cobbled streets, balancing trays of fresh pitta on their heads to be delivered to hummus shops, which are ready with newly-made batches for the breakfast crowd – fishermen, families, and spice and vegetable vendors wanting a filling meal before they set up their stalls for the day.

Up from the harbour is Fisherman's Street, lined on both sides with stainless steel tables where the morning catch is processed: cleaned, sorted by size and quality, then dispatched. The king of the local catch is grouper, a big-lipped predator whose flesh is firm and sweet. The fishermen who have caught one of these can name their price, as any number of fancy Tel Aviv chefs will gladly pay for the privilege of serving it tonight. Local lobster is another treat, as is red snapper. Most of the rest of the catch will be sold in the market to people from all over the Galilee, or to local restaurants which cater to the tourist trade. There are a number of such places in the old fort overlooking the sea, and they all follow the same formula: you order the fish by type, pay by weight, and get it with a salad, fries and a wedge of lemon. The waiter will ask whether you want your fish open or closed (meaning butterflied or on the bone), and grilled or fried. This last is not so much a question as a test; there

is definitely a right or wrong answer, and there are strict rules. Order your bonito fried and you'll be told off by your waiter – bonito goes on the grill. The red mullet, on the other hand, is much nicer fried, making it crispy and sweet. I'm not at all sure why they bother asking.

By noon, or one o'clock at the latest, the shops on Fisherman's Street are empty of produce and being hosed down. Ferocious gangs of street cats fight over the scraps, the heads and guts and any bones that a careless knife has left a morsel of flesh on. We like to arrive late in the morning, when all the creatures nobody else wants are ours on the cheap: local cuttlefish called *savida*, which are too tough to grill or fry, but which soften to sweet submission when slow-cooked in their own juices for a few hours; and tiny little prawns that don't have a lot of meat on them but contain tons of flavour and are delicious fried with garlic and chilli to make a great, crunchy nibble. Best of all is the by-catch – the small fish that are dragged up in the net with the larger ones. The size of a finger or a hand, they are too small to sort individually, so are sold together as a jumble of wonderful shapes, their names a mixture of Arabic, Hebrew, Greek and Ladino (the Judeo-Spanish language spoken by some Sephardic Jews). The skinny little fish with beaks and big side fins are *asfourin* (Arabic for birds); the anchovy-like ones called *hamsi* have five yellow stripes (*hamsa* means five in Arabic); in Hebrew the flat, square ones with big eyes are *televisions* (for obvious reasons); *barbunya* are tiny, sweet red

FISH & SEAFOOD

mullets, using the Greek and Turkish name; and *merluzinos* are little hakes, derived from the Spanish *merluza*. We always used to get a few kilos of by-catch when people were coming over. The fish don't need scaling or gutting, just a little soak in cold salted water before wrapping each one gently in vine or fig leaves for protection and flavour. Then simply secure with a skewer and place on a hot grill for a minute or two. You eat the whole thing, head, tail and bones, chewing carefully. The flavour is second to none.

It's not just the fish shops that are shutting up at midday. The hummus shops traditionally close at noon too – hummus is breakfast food here – though some now stay open later to cater to the tourist trade. Still, by late afternoon, the market will wind down and most shops will be closed, and by dusk the streets are generally quiet. Any residual hubbub will be around the sweet shops selling *baklava* and *knafe*, or outside the kebab shops serving locals who want a night off cooking. This town likes to turn in early.

It's been like this for ever, but slowly things are shifting; the place is becoming gentrified. Many of the romantically-crumbling Ottoman mansions are now being restored and turned into extremely expensive hotels. The Turkish Bazaar has been done up, its pretty shops now selling hand-made pottery and artisan soaps scented with Galilean herbs and sea salt that cost you a small fortune. There's a new type of restaurant too, where the waiters don't ask if you want your fish fried or grilled. You can have it raw with chillies, braised with porcini, or steamed with Galilean wild herbs and sea salt (however you have it, it'll be pricey). In the cobbled alleys you can see signs in Hebrew, English and Arabic beseeching local residents not to sell their properties, to help stop this process. 'Akko is our home!' This town has seen many changes over the centuries of its existence. It has been fought over and ruled by pretty much every major and middling player in the Mediterranean, but to me the true rulers have always been the packs of mean cats who run these streets, and the rude boys on the fort wall, jumping down to the glittering sea for fun.

Grilled salted bass

Enough for 4 people as part of a larger meal (or allow a whole fish per person as dinner)

Brushing the fish with salted water while it cooks helps it stay moist and seasons it really well. At Honey & Smoke we sometimes use this method; at other times we simply brine the fish in plenty of salt water for 20 minutes before grilling, avoiding the constant need to turn and brush it. But brining in advance requires a lot of salt solution, so the following method is a far more home-friendly way of achieving great results. We use bass here simply because we love the delicate flavour, but brine-brushing is a great trick when grilling any whole fish.

2 whole bass (600–800 g / 21–28 oz), gutted and descaled

1 lemon, cut into 8 wedges

4 sprigs of dill

4 sprigs of fresh oregano

100 ml / 3½ fl oz water

1 tbsp sea salt

Use a sharp knife to make a long slit lengthways down the side of each fish. Fill each belly cavity with a couple of lemon wedges, two sprigs of dill and two sprigs of oregano. Heat the water a little and add the salt and the remaining lemon wedges. Stir until all the salt is dissolved.

Brush the salt solution all over the fish, then place them on the BBQ over a high heat. Grill for 2 minutes, then flip them carefully and brush generously with the salt solution. Grill for another 2 minutes before flipping them over and brushing again. Repeat this process three more times, so that the fish cook for 6 minutes each side in total. The skin should now be glistening and tight, and the fish inside fully cooked. Serve hot.

To cook without a BBQ

Place the fish on a rack on top of a roasting tin in a very hot oven (240°C/220°C fan/gas mark 9) and follow the method above for timings, turnings and brine-bastings.

Red mullets with sweet lemon dressing

Allow 1–2 per person, depending on the size of the rest of the meal

Red mullet is possibly our favourite fish and if it is on a menu anywhere, we will most likely order it. It really doesn't need much – a delicious whiff of smoke, a little zingy dressing and dinner is served. 'Red mullet' is also our nickname for our lovely photographer, Patricia, as both she and the fish are adored by us, and both have a great reddish tinge.

4 red mullets (each about 200 g / 7 oz), gutted and descaled

strips of peel from 2 lemons (use a strip zester or peeler)

flaky sea salt

freshly ground black pepper

For the sweet lemon sauce

juice of 2 lemons (the ones you stripped of peel)

2 tbsp sugar

½ tsp flaky sea salt

1 tbsp olive oil

1 small bunch of parsley (about 30 g / 1 oz), finely chopped

Use a sharp knife to make a long slit lengthways down the side of each fish and put a couple of pieces of lemon peel in each belly cavity. Season all over with salt and pepper.

Grill the fish over a high heat for 4 minutes each side. While the fish is grilling, put the lemon juice, sugar, salt and olive oil in a small pan and bring to a boil. Remove from the heat and stir in half the parsley.

As soon as the fish comes off the grill, douse it with the sauce, sprinkle with the remaining parsley and serve straight away.

To cook without a BBQ

Place the fish on a rack on top of a roasting tin in a very hot oven (240°C/220°C fan/gas mark 9) and cook for 4 minutes on each side.

Preserved lemon fish cakes

Makes 6 fish cakes, enough for a meal for 2

Fish cake kebabs (as we call them back home) are a great way to convince fish-queasy family or friends that fish is delicious – no dealing with bones, lots of flavour, a recognizable texture and really simple to cook. The recipe also scales up easily if you're feeding a crowd. It's best to shape and chill the fish cakes before cooking in order to stop them falling apart on the grill. We suggest serving with sliced tomatoes, yogurt, herbs and plenty of lemon juice.

400 g / 14 oz skinless, deboned white fish (use bass, bream, hake or even cod), cut into small cubes
1 small bunch of parsley, leaves picked and chopped (about 20 g / ¾ oz)
1 small bunch of coriander, leaves picked and chopped (about 20 g / ¾ oz)
2 preserved lemons (skin only, discard the pulp), finely chopped (about 20 g / ¾ oz)
3–4 spring onions, finely chopped (about 20 g / ¾ oz)
1 egg
1 tsp ground fennel seeds
1 tsp ground coriander
1 tsp table salt
2 tbsp breadcrumbs
a little vegetable oil for shaping

Combine all the ingredients for the fish cakes, apart from the oil, and knead thoroughly until everything binds together well. Coat your palms with some oil and form the mixture into six round, slightly-flattened patties. Place on a plate in the fridge to firm up for at least an hour before cooking.

Carefully place the fish cakes on the grill over a really hot BBQ and cook for 3 minutes each side before serving.

To cook without a BBQ

Use a lightly oiled, preheated griddle pan on your stove and cook just as you would on the fire.

Salmon on the grill with egg and dill sauce

Dinner for two

2 salmon fillets, skin-on

a little olive oil, for brushing

½ tsp ground fennel seeds

½ tsp flaky sea salt

a generous sprinkling of freshly ground black pepper

For the sauce

4 eggs

1 small bunch of dill, finely chopped

3 spring onions, very thinly sliced

3 tbsp vegetable oil

1 tsp Dijon mustard

juice of half a lemon

½ tsp flaky sea salt

Brush the salmon with olive oil and sprinkle with the fennel, salt and pepper. Refrigerate until you are ready to grill.

Boil the eggs for 7 minutes in salted water, then run under a cold tap until cool enough to handle. Peel the eggs and grate coarsely into a small bowl. Add the remaining sauce ingredients and mix well. This sauce tastes best at room temperature, so if you are making it in advance, remember to take it out of the fridge at least an hour before serving.

When you are ready to eat, grill the fish flesh-side down on a hot BBQ for 3 minutes, then flip the fillets over to finish cooking skin-side down for 4 minutes. Remove to serving plates and accompany with the egg sauce.

This dish is also really tasty eaten cold, if you have any leftovers or want to serve it as part of a picnic or buffet.

To cook without a BBQ

Use a lightly oiled, preheated griddle pan on your stove and cook just as you would on the fire. Or you could simply use a non-stick frying pan.

Birds

Chicken was the most common meat that we encountered on our travels around the Eastern Mediterranean. Chickens were most likely first domesticated more than 10,000 years ago in Asia, and chicken-rearing in the Middle East really took off when the ancient Egyptians discovered they could incubate eggs without a hen.

The widespread availability of this cheap, lean, easy-to-cook protein means that chickens remain a major food source in the Mediterranean, bred both for their eggs and their meat.

It is important to buy a high-quality bird to produce a good meal – ideally choose free-range, and certainly not a cheap battery-farmed one. A decent chicken can easily produce a meal for four, so it is worth paying a decent price. Look for plump flesh, no smell, and a taut, shiny skin, preferably buying from a provenance that you trust.

If you can get a whole chicken complete with offal, make sure you use every last part of the bird: freeze the lovely livers, hearts and gizzards each time until you have enough to make a dish of them (a hugely popular meal in the Middle East); use the necks to make the best chicken stock ever; and save the little pocket of fat from the cavity to add to your next batch of roast potatoes.

Pigeon and squab (unfledged pigeon) are also very popular in the Levant, and are traditionally boiled and stuffed before grilling. Duck is less common, but we did sometimes see it for sale in food markets, especially in Egypt. You will find one recipe using each of these birds in this chapter, showcasing how their flavour really benefits from cooking over fire and smoke. However, the majority of the recipes are for chicken, with the aim of giving you a number of very different ways of cooking this lovely bird on the grill, from marinated and skewered to brined and roasted whole. This may well turn out to be the chapter you use the most.

BIRDS

Thessaloniki, Greece: Late lunch

Our friends, a restaurateur and a wine maker, were coming to meet us, driving up from Halkidiki, the three-pronged peninsula south of Thessaloniki. They had told us that we must visit this place a short drive from town, where the chef does amazing things with fire.

We drove to Kallipoli, a little village at the foot of the Vermio and Paiko mountains. The restaurant was a small house that looked as welcoming as a home. We walked through a generous front garden with tables and chairs set out beneath the fruit trees, past a big wood-fired oven, and into a simple room, cosy, warm and barely decorated. The kitchen was off to the side with a large, open hearth along one wall. It contained an enormous custom-made grill, with various-sized racks, levers that could be adjusted to set the best cooking distance from the heat, and hooks above it for slow cooking or cold smoking – an impressive piece of kit; a chef's dream come true. On the counter nearby were a few loaves of freshly baked bread, golden and fragrant. This was clearly the heart of the place.

We had some time before our companions were due to arrive, so we sat outside under an orange tree. It was late lunchtime on a weekday, in a sleepy village, so Vasilis the chef had plenty of time to chat to us. It turned out he used to live in London; he'd even worked in the same restaurant that we once had. He had joined several years after we left, but we still knew plenty of people in common. We slipped straight into kitchen gossip, the biggest pleasure of all, discussing the crazy pastry chef, that eternal sous chef, the neurotic receptionist.

A Thessaloniki boy, Vasilis grew up in the town but work took him travelling. First to the islands, working the busy season, the three summer months that are all about cooking and making money before collapsing, then on to Athens, London, Moscow, and back to the Greek islands. He ran big operations – concept restaurants, hotel kitchens – but his dream was always this: to have a place of his own in the area where he grew up; to be his own boss; to work with the people he loves; to cook with the local produce he cherishes; and to build the kick-ass grill he always wanted. His wife grew up in this village, and she and her sister work here together, sharing the cooking, cleaning and serving. Their parents still live next door.

We told him our story, too: how we came to London from Israel, only meaning to stay a couple of months, but ending up falling in love with it, and how it is home now. We told him about each of our jobs since we left that place by the river overlooking St. Paul's and the Gherkin; how we too wanted a place of our own in our new home town, where we could be our own bosses, work only with people we love, with the best produce we can find, cooking on a kick-ass grill – and how we finally managed to get there. We didn't need to tell one another how great all of it is, how we each had got exactly what we wanted, how the huge challenges and huge sacrifices along the way were, and are, still all worth it.

Our companions arrived in true Greek manner: about three hours late, loud, and bringing with them kids, in-laws, friends, dogs, bottles of wine

and plenty of stories. The food we were served had a simple sophistication which showed that rare combination of skill and humility. A dish of potatoes from the garden next door, cut into discs, grilled simply and dressed with local oil, local honey, sea salt and thyme flowers – clean, simple flavours, so delicious. Home-cured ham came next, with sun-warmed vine tomatoes grown by the chef's father-in-law, the combination naturally salty and sweet, needing nothing else. Best of all was the chicken: a simple roast bird with bronzed, crisp skin and moist, savoury, smoky flesh. When we asked the secret of it, the first thing Vasilis said (before he explained his process) was that he gets very good chickens – always the correct answer.

By the end of the afternoon our group was the only one left. The sisters were in the kitchen, washing-up and getting ready for dinner service, chatting and laughing, working together in comfortable familiarity. The chef was having a short break, stretching his legs and smoking a cigarette. He joined us for a glass of wine and we showered him with compliments.

We didn't want to leave. Over bitter coffee and sweet apple *baklava* we looked at the family in the kitchen, scrubbing, chopping and chatting, and we saw ourselves. The hard graft, the long hours, the stress – these all seem insignificant when you get to do the work you love with the people you love. We hope that the guests in our restaurants feel as welcomed, happy and well-looked after as we felt at that moment.

Whole roast chicken – cooked 2 ways

Using a 1.5 kg / 3 lb 5 oz bird, to feed 3–4 guests

Chickens can vary from a light-weight 1 kg / 2 lb 4 oz to a whopping 2.5 kg / 5½ lb, so please take this into account when cooking and serving. If feeding more than four people, we tend to cook a second bird. Leftovers are never a problem as we love to eat them the next day in a salad or sandwich. The other thing to consider is who gets which cut: should everyone have a piece of dark meat and a piece of white, or do you fight? For us it's clear: brown meat for Sarit, white breast meat for Itamar, and a wing each – they are a treat. Brining the chicken the evening before roasting will ensure moist and succulent meat with very little chance of overcooking, so we strongly advise you try it. You can re-use the brine within a couple of days, as long as you have kept it in the fridge in the meantime.

For the aromatic brine

2 lt / 3 ½ pints water
6 tbsp table salt
4 bay leaves
2 tbsp whole black peppercorns
1 small bunch of thyme
4 strips of lemon skin
2 garlic cloves, halved

Stir the brining ingredients together until the salt has completely dissolved.

If you are using the spatchcock method (page 134), you will need to prepare the bird before brining. Don't worry if you haven't done this before – it's simple. Place it breast-side down on a chopping board and use a sturdy pair of scissors or a sharp knife to cut along either side of the backbone. Remove the spine, then flip the bird over so the ribcage is facing down. Press hard on the breastbone (as if you were giving CPR) to crush the ribcage flat, then spread the legs out to the sides. You can make the flattening process easier by removing the wishbone with a small knife first, but I don't usually bother.

Put the (whole or flattened) chicken in a large, deep tray or bowl and pour the brine over to cover it entirely. Refrigerate for at least 12 hours and up to 24 hours. Remove the chicken from the brine and pat dry.

Spit-roasted with honey-garlic butter

1 lovely bird, about 1.5 kg / 3 lb 5 oz, brined for at least 12 hours

1 lemon, halved

50 g / 1¾ oz butter

3 tbsp honey

3 garlic cloves, peeled and minced

1 tbsp ground cumin

freshly ground black pepper

Place the lemon halves in the bird's cavity then insert a long purpose-built spit (or a long skewer) through the cavity, spitting the bird from top to tail. If you are using a spit-roaster with an automatic rotating handle, then nothing could be easier: simply place it above a hot BBQ and start it rolling. If you are using the long skewer instead, you will have to rotate the chicken manually every 8 minutes. Use two large concrete blocks (or a metal frame or wire at either end of the BBQ) to suspend the skewered bird securely above the heat.

While the chicken starts cooking, melt the butter in a small pan. Stir in the honey, garlic, cumin and black pepper and mix well. After the chicken has been turning for about 25 minutes, start brushing it at 8-minute intervals with the honey-garlic butter. Do this four times, roasting it for another 32 minutes in total, and then test it by inserting a knife into the thickest part of the thigh. If the juices run clear with no sign of blood, then you are almost ready to serve. Remove from the grill and leave to rest for 10 minutes, before carving and devouring.

To cook without a BBQ

It's tricky to have a spit roast without an open fire or a BBQ; easier to just cook the bird in the oven. Rub the honey-garlic butter all over the chicken, pop it in a roasting tin and roast at 220°C/200°C fan/gas mark 7 for 45–50 minutes, basting twice as it cooks, until the juices from the thickest part of the thigh run clear. Then leave to rest in the oven with the heat turned off for 10 minutes before serving.

Spatchcocked with Mediterranean spices

3 tbsp ras el hanout spice (see recipe on page 218)

1 tbsp sumac

½ tsp freshly ground black pepper

3 tbsp olive oil

1 lovely bird, about 1.5 kg / 3 lb 5 oz, spatchcocked and brined for at least 12 hours

Mix the spices with the olive oil to form a thick paste. Place the flattened bird skin-side down on the grill over a medium-low heat and brush some of the spice paste onto the exposed cavity. Leave to cook for 10 minutes, then flip the bird and brush the skin-side with spice paste. Grill for 10 minutes before flipping it again and applying more paste. Repeat four more times, grilling for about an hour in total, turning and basting the bird every 10 minutes. Keep an eye on the coals – you want them to provide a nice mellow heat throughout, so you may need to top them up a little as you go.

Test the chicken by inserting a knife into the thickest part of the thigh. If the juices run clear with no sign of blood, then you are almost ready to serve. Remove from the grill and leave to rest for 10 minutes, before carving and devouring.

To cook without a BBQ

Colour the bird skin-side down in a lightly oiled, preheated griddle pan over a medium heat for 10 minutes, then flip it over. Baste the skin-side generously with all the spice paste and transfer the chicken to a roasting tray. Roast at 220°C/200°C fan/gas mark 7 for 35 minutes, or until the juices from the thickest part of the thigh run clear. Turn the oven off and leave the bird inside to rest for 10 minutes before serving.

Chicken kofta with tzatziki and flatbread

Makes 18–20 small kofta

You can make the kofta a day ahead and rest them in the fridge until you are ready to cook, or even freeze the shaped patties for up to a month (just make sure they are completely thawed before grilling). We usually make our own mince from chicken thighs as we find it tastier and juicier, but shop-bought chicken (or turkey) mince works just fine too. You use the bulb-end of the spring onions in the kofta and the leaf-end in the tzatziki, so there's no wastage – plus the two taste great together, making them natural partners.

For the kofta

1 kg / 2 lb 4 oz chicken mince

150 g / 5¼ oz feta cheese, crumbled

1 egg

2 tbsp breadcrumbs

½ tsp baking powder

½ tsp table salt

plenty of freshly ground black pepper

5–6 spring onions, white parts only (about 50 g / 1¾ oz), finely chopped (green parts go in the tzatziki)

¾ large bunch of dill, chopped (about 30 g / 1 oz)

3–4 sprigs of fresh oregano, finely chopped (about 10 g / ⅓ oz), or 1 tsp dried

zest of 1 lime (use the juice on the cooked kofta)

Work all the kofta ingredients together until fully combined. You may want to oil your palms lightly before shaping them, as it's a sticky business; I usually set a small bowl of oil next to a tray before I start. Form the mixture into 18–20 little patties, each about 60–70 g / 2¼–2½ oz, placing them on the tray as you go. Wash your hands really well before covering the kofta with some cling film and placing in the fridge to chill for at least an hour, and up to 24 hours, before grilling.

When you are ready to cook, get your BBQ to a medium heat so that you can get a good colour on the kofta, but not risk burning them before they are done. Place the patties on the grill and cook for about 5–6 minutes on each side, until really springy to touch. Remove from the heat and squeeze the lime juice all over them while they are still hot. Serve with the tzatziki and plenty of flatbread (see recipe on page 220).

For the tzatziki

250 g / 9 oz full fat Greek-style yogurt

about 30 g / 1 oz spring onion, green parts only, finely chopped (white parts go in the kofta)

¼ large bunch of dill, chopped (about 10 g / ⅓ oz)

1 clove of garlic, peeled and minced or grated

zest and juice of 1 lime

200 g / 7 oz cucumber, roughly grated

3 tbsp olive oil

½ tsp flaky sea salt

Squeeze the grated cucumber to remove excess liquid and mix with the other tzatziki ingredients. Store in the fridge until needed. This keeps well for a couple of days.

To cook without a BBQ

Bake the kofta in a very hot oven (240°C/220°C fan/gas mark 9) for 10–12 minutes, or use a preheated griddle pan on your stove and cook just as you would on the fire.

Chicken shish in sweet confit garlic marinade

Makes 6 skewers

The amount of garlic in the marinade may seem a little excessive at first, but please do try it, as the sweet, delicate flavour is simply fantastic. You don't want to lose this by burning it, so it is really important to grill these skewers over a gentle heat. This is a great recipe to make ahead, as you can confit the garlic cloves a day or two in advance of making the marinade, and marinate the chicken for up to 48 hours before cooking.

800 g / 1¾ lb skinless, boneless chicken thighs, cut into large pieces (or left whole if oven-roasting)

For the confit garlic

1–2 heads of garlic, broken into cloves but unpeeled (about 150 g / 5¼ oz)

100 ml / 3½ fl oz vegetable oil

For the marinade

1 batch of confit garlic cloves

3–4 tbsp garlicky confit oil

1 small bunch of parsley, chopped

1 heaped tsp flaky sea salt

a few twists of freshly ground black pepper

zest of ½ lemon (use the juice on the cooked chicken shish)

Place the unpeeled garlic cloves in a small pan or metal tray and cover with the oil. You may need a touch more, depending on the size of the pan – it should be enough to just cover the cloves. Set on the side of the grill where there is the lowest heat (or set it over a very low heat on the stove) and slowly bring to a boil. Once bubbles start to appear, cook for 10 minutes, then remove from the heat and set aside in the pan to soften and cool entirely. You can store the cooled garlic and oil in the fridge for up to 48 hours before using.

To make the marinade, lift the cooled cloves out of the oil (retaining it for later) and squeeze to pop the flesh out of the skins and into a small bowl. Discard the skins. Use the back of a spoon to smash the confit garlic into a pulp, then stir in the chopped parsley, salt, pepper, lemon zest and 3–4 tablespoons of the garlicky oil. Pour over the chicken pieces, mix well to coat, then thread the meat onto skewers. Place in the fridge and leave to marinate for anything from 1 hour to 48 hours.

When you are ready to cook, get the BBQ nice and mellow. Grill the skewers for 5 minutes on one side, then flip and cook for 5 minutes on the other side. Dab any remaining marinade or, if there's none left, some garlicky confit oil on the chicken, then flip once more and cook for a final 5 minutes. Remove from the grill and squeeze the lemon juice all over them before serving.

Joojeh kebabs
– chicken in yogurt and saffron

Makes 4 large skewers (allow at least one per person)

8 large chicken thighs (boneless and skinless
– about 1.2 kg / 2 lb 10 oz net weight)

For the marinade

1 onion, peeled (about 150 g / 5¼ oz)

3 garlic cloves, peeled

1 green chilli, halved and seeds removed

2 tbsp ras el hanout spice mix (see page 218)

2 tsp salt

½ tsp turmeric

zest from 1 lemon

1 pinch of saffron strands

1 tbsp rose water

80 ml / 2¾ fl oz water

200 g / 7 oz goats' yogurt

Purée the onion, garlic and chilli together in a food processor. Transfer to a large bowl, then combine with the rest of the marinade ingredients. Add the chicken thighs and mix really well to coat all over. Leave to marinate for at least 2 hours and up to 24 hours.

When you are ready to cook, use double skewers for each kebab (to keep the thighs as flat as possible) and thread with two pieces of marinated chicken. Keep any remaining marinade to baste the chicken as it is grilling.

Roast over good hot coals to caramelize the marinade and develop the sweetness, turning the kebabs every 5 minutes and brushing with leftover marinade after each turn. The chicken will take about 15–20 minutes to cook through. If your BBQ has a lid, covering it for 5 minutes will help the kebabs cook well without charring too much; however, we tend not to do this as we really favour the taste of the charred marinade.

Serve with a small herb salad mixed with orange segments, for a freshness that goes really well with the robust marinade.

To cook without a BBQ

Roast the chicken thighs (no need to skewer them) in a very hot oven (240°C/220°C fan/gas mark 9) for 15–20 minutes, or use a lightly oiled, preheated griddle pan on your stove and cook just as you would on the fire.

Petra & Wadi Rum, Jordan: *Zarb*

It could be claimed that Petra is Jordan's second city, and its streets are probably as busy today as they were when it was inhabited by the Nabataeans more than 2,000 years ago. On the day that we visited it seemed as if the majority of the population was Malaysian, although there were tourists from all over the world. Like any major city, Petra has its own transport system; this consists mainly of donkeys or horses pulling carts driven by cigarette-smoking, kohl-wearing boys, who will take you down the *Siq*, the twisting, narrow gorge that leads to the famous treasury, *Al Khazneh*. Even if you have seen a thousand pictures, nothing really prepares you for how breathtaking it is. A perfectly proportioned palace leaps out at you from the rose-tinted stones, its columns and elaborate decorations delicately carved all those centuries ago. This is downtown Petra, where you can sit and have a drink in the main square, and do some people watching, if you can tear your eyes away from the carved façades. There are stalls selling snacks and souvenirs, including make-up. The famous eye kohl, used by men as well as women, was traditionally made of ground desert rock, but if you look carefully at what's on sale here, it says 'Made in China' (Petra has always been a global trade centre). There is a pharmacy of sorts, selling desert medicine, and even a book store that only stocks one title – *Married to a Bedouin*, written and sold by a Kiwi woman who was, well, married to a

Bedouin (something the guidebooks to the region advise against). You can spend days exploring this magical city, still so vibrant today, and it is not at all hard to imagine what life must have been like here all those centuries ago, how the citizens lived, loved and worked, what they did for fun, what they ate…

If you make it to Petra, you might as well spend the night in Wadi Rum. Pretty much everyone does. This valley in the desert is one of the most bewitching places on earth, a soft sea of sand from which rise rocky outcrops layered in psychedelic colours – reds, purples and greens – like the sunset solidified into rock. The Bedouin camps here are probably some of the most cosmopolitan places in the Middle East; people come from all over the world: hippies and dreamers and desert souls; hikers and bikers; adrenaline junkies; and peace-seekers keen to join moonlit mindfulness sessions or do yoga at sunrise.

At night the Bedouin hosts make a big show of cooking *zarb*. A fire is lit in a deep pit in the sand and, when the flames have settled, metal racks laden with chicken and vegetables are lowered on top of the brightly glowing coals. The pit is covered with a lid, onto which sand is heaped to seal it.

While the food slowly cooks in that hot, smoky chamber, something magical happens, a strange alchemy. Gradually the noise of the camp dies down; at last it's time for the show. Two

Bedouins are the masters of ceremony, looking the part in their traditional black dress and red headscarves. They take a shovel to the pit to uncover it, and suddenly, with a great puff of smoke, the lid is off, a glow emanating from the ground in the dark desert night as the laden racks are lifted out. The smell is incredible – smoke and meat, desert herbs and hot sand – as, with great pomp, everything is carried inside the tent for all to share the feast. Our hosts play music and dance, some Russians join in, then a group from Argentina… This show happens every night here. Every night there is a party and, even though we know it's all staged for us tourists, it is still winning our hearts. It is all still completely magical.

We take our plates outside. The air has a chill to it but warmth still rises from the sand. In the night sky the moon and stars shine so brightly it almost seems like day, and the desert sand that was a dull ochre a few hours ago is now a sea of silver. We eat with our fingers. All the flavours of the food seem to have been intensified by the stay in that underground oven: the carrots are sweeter, the meat meatier; you can certainly taste the smoke, and maybe something else as well. It is easy to get mystical in the desert night, but it feels like eating the essence of the place – the sand, the rocks, the sun – and we imagine the original residents of Petra sitting just like us, under the brilliant sky, eating *zarb*.

BIRDS

Zarb – hot smoked chicken with root vegetables

A family meal for 4–6

The best thing about making *zarb* is really the extraordinary way in which you cook it – basically, for hours and hours over burning embers, in a metal bin which has been buried in a massive hole in the ground. The food is suspended above the coals in a wire rack. This can be any kind of rack or even a large colander, but the best (and, we think, funniest) is a tiered wire vegetable stand – just don't ever expect to store veggies in it again.

1 chicken (about 1.5 kg / 3 lb 5 oz), divided into 8 (or simply use 8 large thighs)

4 carrots, peeled and cut in 6 cm / 2½ inch pieces

4 potatoes, peeled and cut in large wedges

2 onions, peeled and quartered

3 tbsp vegetable oil

2 tbsp table salt

1 tsp freshly ground black pepper

2 tbsp ground cumin

1 tbsp ground allspice (pimento)

You will need a clean, metal, lidded bin (or drum) in which to cook the food. Dig a hole in the ground that can fit the bin and start a fire in the base (ideally use wood for the best flavour) and leave it to settle into glowing embers. Place all the ingredients in a very large bowl and mix really well to coat the chicken and vegetables with the spices and oil. Transfer the food to your chosen cooking rack, placing the chicken pieces skin-side up with the vegetables nestled in between (in a single layer, if possible).

Slide the rack into the metal bin, cover tightly with the lid, and heap the earth you dug out to make the hole back on top. Leave for 4 hours.

Use a shovel to move the earth off of the lid – don't use your hands as it will get hotter the closer you get to the lid. Use a brush to dust any remaining soil from the lid (you don't want earth falling into your dinner) and use a cloth to remove the lid. Carefully lift the hot rack out of the metal bin, and serve immediately.

To cook without a fire pit

No way José.

Whole chicken and wheat *poike*

Enough for 4–6 to share

Potjiekos or, as we call it in Israel, *poike* is a dish prepared in a traditional South African, three-legged, cast-iron pot (a *potjie*) that sits in the fire. These have become increasingly popular in Israel over the last 15 years and now every household seems to own one. You can see families on the beach with a *potjie* sitting on the fire; when everyone has had a swim and a rest in the sun, dinner will be ready. It makes total sense really: like the Sabbath low-and-slow cooking that is an integral part of Jewish religion and tradition, this pot creates the same lovely combination of comfort food and sensational flavour, and it all happens without too much effort. The only thing you need to do is prepare your ingredients, including soaking the grain for 3–4 hours in advance to soften it. Then simply pop everything in the *potjie* and take it wherever you go – on a trek, to the beach, or simply into your backyard. When you are settled, pop it on the fire and let it work its magic. If you can't get your hands on a *potjie*, use a Dutch oven with a tight-fitting lid and simply elevate it above the fire on a BBQ rack.

1 whole chicken (about 1.5 kg / 3 lb 5 oz)

a handful of celery leaves and/or outer cauliflower leaves, to line the bottom of the pot and stop the food burning

For the wheat and vegetable filling

250 g / 9 oz whole freekeh or wheat berries, soaked for about 3–4 hours

3 sticks of celery, diced (about 100 g / 3½ oz)

1 onion, peeled and diced (about 100 g / 3½ oz)

1 large turnip, peeled and diced (about 100 g / 3½ oz)

½ small cauliflower, roughly chopped (about 150 g / 5¼ oz)

10 large sage leaves, roughly chopped

3 sprigs of rosemary, leaves picked

2 tbsp baharat spice mix (see recipe on page 218)

1 tbsp table salt

Drain the soaked grains and mix with the other filling ingredients. Stuff as much as you can into the cavity of the chicken. Lay the celery leaves and/or cauliflower leaves in the bottom of the *potjie* (or Dutch oven) and sprinkle with a couple of handfuls of the remaining filling. Put the stuffed chicken on top and follow with the rest of the wheat and vegetable mixture. Add just enough water to cover the whole lot and place the lid on tightly.

Set the pot on the fire and leave to cook for an hour before removing the lid and checking the water level. If lots of liquid has formed, cook with the lid off for about half an hour to reduce it a little, then re-cover and cook for another hour and a half. If, after the first hour, the liquid is still at roughly the same level as when you started cooking, keep the *potjie* covered and simply leave to cook for a further 2 hours. Once it has had 3 hours in total, remove from the heat and serve directly from the pot.

To cook without a BBQ

Prepare the dish in a Dutch oven or cast-iron casserole pot with a tightly-fitting lid. Place in the oven at 200°C/180°C fan/gas mark 6 for an hour then check the liquid level. Add a little water if necessary to keep the chicken fully submerged, then re-cover, reduce the heat to 170°C/150°C fan/gas mark 3–4 and cook for a further hour and a half before serving.

BIRDS

Chicken and Swiss chard *fatayer*

Makes 4 chicken parcels

Fatayer are traditionally little fried pastries made from a pitta-like dough and filled with meat, chicken or wilted greens. At Honey & Smoke we developed a version that combines slow-cooked chicken with garlicky Swiss chard, wrapped in a thin Lebanese flatbread and then grilled. This isn't strictly a BBQ dish, as much of the cooking takes place in the kitchen, but since this is one of the most popular dishes in the restaurant, we honestly felt we had to supply the recipe here.

4 large, thin *markook* flatbreads (or plain griddle bread, see page 220)

a drizzle of olive oil

yogurt for serving (optional)

For the chicken

8 chicken thighs, skin-on and bone-in (about 1 kg / 2 lb 4 oz)

2 tsp table salt

3 tbsp baharat spice mix (see recipe on page 218)

3 large onions, peeled and thinly sliced (about 400 g / 14 oz)

For the chard

1 large bunch of Swiss chard (about 400 g / 14 oz)

3 tbsp olive oil

a generous pinch of flaky sea salt

a generous twist of freshly ground black pepper

2 garlic cloves, finely chopped

Heat your oven to 220°C/200°C fan/gas mark 7. Rub the chicken thighs all over with the salt and spice. Place skin-side up in a roasting tin that can fit all the chicken snugly in one layer, then pop in the oven. After 20 minutes, add the sliced onions to the roasting tin and cover with a lid or aluminium foil. Return to the oven for 30 minutes, then carefully remove the lid/foil, mix everything around and roast for a final 20 minutes.

Remove from the oven and, when cool enough to handle, pull the meat away from the bones, tearing the skin into little pieces. Discard the bones and any cartilage. Mix the meat and skin pieces with the onions and any liquid that has formed in the roasting tin. This can be done up to two days in advance; simply store the cooked chicken in the fridge until needed.

To prepare the Swiss chard, tear the leaves off the stalks, wash well and set aside. Wash, drain and finely dice the stalks. Heat the olive oil in a very large saucepan over a medium heat, add the diced stalks, salt and pepper, and sauté for about 10 minutes or until the stalks are very soft. Stir in the chopped garlic, then add the washed leaves and mix well to combine. Increase the heat to high, cover the pan and cook for about 2 minutes until the greens are wilted, then remove from the heat.

Spread the flatbreads on the work surface. (If they are a bit dry and brittle, dampen them with a little warm water, then heat lightly on the grill to make them more pliable.) Divide the Swiss chard between the flatbreads and top with the chicken and onion mixture. Fold the sides of the breads in, then fold in the top and bottom edges to close the parcel like an envelope. Drizzle with a little olive oil and place the *fatayer* seam-side down on a medium grill – not too close to the charcoal to allow time for the insides to heat slowly while the bread crisps to a lovely charred parcel. It should take about 6 minutes on each side. Carefully remove from the grill and serve hot, with a little yogurt to accompany, if you wish.

To cook without a BBQ

Set the parcels seam-side down on a tray lined with baking paper and brush the tops with oil. Bake in a hot oven (220°C/200°C fan/gas mark 7) for about 15 minutes or until the flatbread wrapping has crisped up nicely, then serve hot with some yogurt, if you fancy it.

Alexandria, Egypt: Pigeon lofts and poultry markets

We wanted to visit the food market. In every town we visit, this is our first port of call, so we asked the clerk at the hotel where it was. He demurred, saying the market was not for tourists. "But we love a market!" we replied. He said there wasn't one, even when a check on the internet revealed there definitely was. "Look, in the old city. How do we get there?"

"No, no," he persisted, "no market this week. Go here, good shops!" We realized he was trying to send us to the smart shopping mall behind the Four Seasons Hotel, so we gave up and headed out, walking in the direction of the old city. We were bound to find it soon.

All we did was follow the ladies with the empty shopping bags; the ones with full baskets were clearly on their way back. After a while we passed a man with a small handcart laden with Cape gooseberries (also known as physalis or goldenberry), then a man with a larger cart piled high with breads… we could feel it was getting closer, and eventually the market showed itself in all its grit and glory.

We admired beautiful in-season artichokes; bottles and jars of pickles in all shapes and sizes; and mounds of fluorescent orange, yellow and green citrus fruit arranged in neat pyramids (this is Egypt after all). But walking around the souk district of Alexandria, you cannot miss the animals. There are stacks of large crates and in them creatures are arranged, from the largest at the bottom to the smallest at the top. In one ground-level crate we saw four white ducks; in the next one up were two feisty roosters, separated by wire so they could not fight; and above them were hens, nestling closely together, a sea of brown feathers with yellow eyes. On the top floor were the pigeons, all greys and whites, gently cooing. Next to this poultry condominium was a platform lined with hay, covered with rabbits of all colours and sizes, hopping about, nibbling on their greens. They showed no desire to jump off the platform into the busy market, but simply sat there, content.

Shoppers surveying this menagerie point to their choice – a fluffy-tailed rabbit, a plump pigeon or two – but these are no pets; the adorable bunny will not be handed to a happy, smiling child. Instead the stallholder will pull the unlucky animal out of its group by its legs and take it to the back of the stall, where it will be killed, prepared and, occasionally, cooked on the spot. This is not the kind of store we are used to at all – a real live butcher's shop and delicatessen.

Seeing all the animals about to be turned into fresh meat was a bit startling, even for us chefs. Through supreme effort we in the West have managed to distance ourselves from the brutal part of the process – the gore, the blood, the feathers. We have made it easy for ourselves to forget all that as we look at mouth-watering images of food on social media and in (ahem) fancy cookbooks. Our meat comes to us in neat, hermetically-sealed plastic packs, the cuts displayed in polite burgundies, pinks and whites on a supermarket shelf. Because of this, we eat more meat. And meat is cheaper than ever before.

The smell of live animals, and of dead animals, is the smell of life, an elemental thing we should all know and be comfortable with; as comfortable as we are with eating them for dinner. The people here, adults and children, are not startled, they are not disgusted. What started off as one bird out of many in a cage is now lunch; it had feathers and now it doesn't; it was alive and now it isn't. It goes on the grill and the smell is good, delicious and wholesome; but it is fundamentally still the same thing.

Egyptians are comfortable living alongside their meals. It is not uncommon for people to have a rabbit hutch in their backyard, so that, on special occasions, fresh rabbit meat can be added to slippery, bitter, green *molokhia* (jute) leaves, to make a stew that is a strong contender for the national dish of Egypt. Usually made with water or stock, the addition of rabbit pieces, bones and all, turns it into something decidedly more luxurious.

Many of the flat roofs around the city have a small square structure on top, usually painted in bright colours and bold patterns. These are pigeon lofts. Some of the birds are raised for sport, but most are destined for the table. Out of town, by the side of the road, you can see tall, domed mud structures, pocked with holes forming intricate patterns. These too are pigeon houses, altogether larger, grander affairs than the rooftop versions. Pigeon is much-loved in Egypt; the Egyptians call it *faket al lahma*, the fruit of meat. Traditionally, they are stuffed with spiced rice, boiled till the meat is soft and the rice cooked, and then finished on the grill or in a hot oven.

The meat on these little birds is intensely flavoured, deeply savoury and slightly sweet, and this dish is the height of Egyptian cuisine, reserved for high days and special occasions. Rice is ubiquitous here, and delicious – short plump grains with a floral scent and the most delightful bite. Grown in the Nile Delta, it is served with almost every meal, and indeed it is so important to the national diet that there's a ban on export, to prevent shortages and price hikes.

We meandered around the market, buying neither vegetables nor fruit, and certainly not poultry or rabbits. Instead we bought spices, pickles and tahini fresh from the mill, things that we would be able to carry surreptitiously through the hotel lobby under the snooty gaze of the receptionist, and stuff into our suitcase to take home. The hubbub of the market died down around us as the stalls were packed up. We watched as a man with a crate full of ducks opened a door in a

back alley, releasing the birds into the courtyard beyond. In that courtyard in the middle of town, surrounded by apartments, was a miniature farm – chickens and ducks pecking and scratching around for a bite to eat, bunnies hopping about. It was far from any image of a rural idyll, but here in Alexandria this is what organic, free-range farming looks like.

Smoked duck breast with pickled cherries and cashew cream

A main for 2 or a great starter for 4

Salting the duck in advance brings the meaty flavour to the fore and helps keep it moist during the smoking and cooking. The layer of fat melts and gives a luxurious feel to every mouthful. We serve the duck with pickled cherries – the fruit provides a sweet, sharp, acidic contrast to the rich, savoury meat – and with a lavish cashew cream. The cherries and cashew cream need a little advance planning (3 days for the cherries, 1 day for the cashews) so if you are short of time, or simply can't be bothered with the accompaniments, just give the smoked duck a try; it is well worth it.

For the pickled cherries

100 ml / 3½ fl oz red wine vinegar
100 ml / 3½ fl oz water
40 g / 1½ oz dark brown sugar
½ tsp flaky sea salt
1 star anise
1 whole clove
1 bay leaf
6 whole black peppercorns
250 g / 9 oz whole cherries

The above method makes a full jar, more than you need for this recipe, but they will keep well and can be used in salads or as a nibble with cheese or cured meats. Bring the vinegar, water, sugar, salt and spices to the boil, then leave to cool to room temperature. Sterilize a clean jar by popping it in a hot oven (200°C/180°C fan/gas mark 6) for 5 minutes before filling; alternatively pour boiling water in and leave for 10 seconds before tipping the water out and using immediately. Put the cherries in the sterilized jar and pour the pickling liquor over. Seal and set aside in a cool, dark cupboard or pantry for three days before transferring them to the fridge to stop them over-pickling.

For the cashew cream

120 g / 4¼ oz raw cashews, soaked overnight in cold water
1 large clove of garlic, peeled
juice of ½ lemon
1–2 generous pinches of flaky sea salt

Drain most, but not all, of the water from the nuts. Put 3 tablespoons of the soaking water along with the cashews in a blender (ideally a really powerful one like a Vitamix or Thermomix) and blitz to a smooth paste. Add the garlic clove, lemon juice and salt, and blend to a nice thick purée, then sprinkle in a little cold water, a few drops at a time, and blitz until you have a lovely custard-like cream.

For the duck breasts

2 duck breasts (about 220 g / 8 oz each)
1 tbsp flaky sea salt
1 tbsp brown sugar
½ tsp mild chilli flakes
½ tsp roughly crushed pink peppercorns
½ tsp crushed fennel seeds

Use a sharp knife to score the duck skin in a criss-cross pattern. Mix the salt, sugar, chilli flakes, peppercorns and crushed fennel seeds together and sprinkle over both sides of the duck breasts. Set on a plate, cover and place in the fridge for at least 30 minutes and up to 4 hours.

When you are ready to cook, remove the duck from the fridge and dab dry with some paper towel. Place skin-side up on a small rack.

To smoke the duck over the BBQ in its initial stages, set up the charcoal or wood with plenty of wood chips scattered around, put the duck on its rack directly over it, and light the fire. Cover the breasts with a deep lid or a metal bowl, and leave to sit in the smoke from the newly-lit fire for about 8 minutes.

Remove the lid and put the duck skin-side down in a frying pan. Place the pan on the now settled charcoal at a medium heat and render the fat from the breasts. Cook the skin till it is very crisp, about 6–8 minutes, occasionally emptying any fat that accumulates into a small dish. Then flip the breasts over and sauté for 4–5 minutes on the other side. Cover the frying pan with aluminium foil and leave to rest at the side of the BBQ for about 10 minutes, before slicing and serving, ideally accompanied by the pickled cherries and cashew cream.

To smoke and cook without a BBQ

Place a couple of burning coals (or some lighted wood chips) in a roasting tin containing the contents of 1 tea bag or 1 heaped teaspoon of dried tea leaves and a handful of wood chips. Place a rack over the tray. Once the tea and woodchips are smouldering, place the breast on the rack skin-side up, cover the tray with aluminium foil and set aside to smoke for 10 minutes. Remove the duck from the smoker and cook in a frying pan on the stove over a medium heat.

BIRDS

Grilled pigeon with onion and pine nut jam

Dinner for 4

In Egypt pigeons play an important role not only as food, but also in sport. Many homes have a pigeon house on the roof and the birds are reared for racing as well as for dinner. The breed of pigeon we ate there has much lighter meat than the birds we get in Europe, less gamey and closer to quail in flavour. Egyptian pigeon is usually served well-done, often boiled in broth then stuffed with flavoured rice and grilled, but the likelihood of getting your butcher to source Middle Eastern pigeon is slim, so we adapted the recipe for our restaurant using British game or European farmed birds. These are better served really rare, otherwise they can become tough and gamey. The onion jam is delicious served warm with the grilled pigeon, but it also keeps really well in the fridge for a week or so, so you can enjoy any leftovers with some sharp cheese and crackers.

4 whole pigeons, plucked, gutted and cleaned (you can do this yourself but much easier to ask the butcher)

For the marinade

1 tsp finely chopped rosemary leaves

2 tbsp olive oil

a pinch of freshly ground black pepper

¼ tsp ground allspice (pimento)

¼ tsp ground cinnamon

1 tsp flaky sea salt

For the onion and pine nut jam

4 tbsp olive oil

4 large onions, peeled and thinly sliced lengthways from root to tip (about 500 g / 1 lb 2 oz)

1 tsp flaky sea salt

1 tbsp dark brown sugar

50 g / 1¾ oz golden raisins, soaked in plenty of cold water for a couple of hours

50 g / 1¾ oz pine nuts, lightly roasted

1 cinnamon stick

½ tsp ground allspice (pimento)

a generous pinch of freshly ground black pepper

a pinch of chilli flakes

Place each bird breast-side down and use a sturdy pair of scissors or a sharp knife to cut along either side of the backbone. Remove the spine and open the bird up so that you can dab it dry inside and out with kitchen paper.

Mix the marinade ingredients together and brush all over the pigeons, including inside the cavity. Place in the fridge to marinate for at least 1 hour and up to 24 hours.

To cook the jam, heat the olive oil in a large frying pan over a medium heat. Add the sliced onions and salt, and cook slowly for about 30 minutes, stirring occasionally. Stir in the remaining ingredients and reduce the heat to low. Allow to cook really slowly for another 20 minutes until the onions are dark and really soft.

When you are ready to cook, make sure the fire has mellowed to a medium heat and set the cooking rack a little away above the embers. Grill the pigeons on one breast for 5 minutes, then turn them to grill the other breast for 5 minutes too. Finally flip them breast-side up (so the cavity is facing the fire) to cook for 8 more minutes before removing from the heat. Cover them with aluminium foil and leave to rest for 5 minutes before serving with the warm onion jam.

To cook without a BBQ

Heat a good amount of oil in a large, heavy-bottomed (oven-proof) skillet and fry the pigeons on one side for about 6 minutes. Flip them over to fry the other side for 6 minutes too, then turn them breast-side up and pop the whole skillet in the oven at 200°C/180°C fan/gas mark 6 for 8 minutes. Remove from the oven, cover the pan with aluminium foil and leave to rest for 10 minutes before serving with the warm onion jam.

Chicken wings in spicy pomegranate molasses

**About 8–12 wings
(allow 3–4 per person)**

1 kg / 2 lb 4 oz chicken wings, halved at the joint and small wingtips removed

For the marinade

1 red chilli, finely sliced

3 spring onions, finely sliced

1 tbsp sweet paprika

1 tbsp smoked paprika

4 tbsp pomegranate molasses

2 tbsp olive oil

1 tsp freshly ground black pepper

1 tbsp flaky sea salt

Mix all the marinade ingredients together, then stir in the chicken wings. You can cook them straight away, but they taste even better if you leave them to marinate in the fridge for 6–8 hours.

When you are ready to grill, it is best to pop the wings in a flat grilling basket

(the kind you would use to barbecue small fish) to hold them evenly in one layer and keep them secure. Use the remaining marinade for basting.

Place the grilling basket on the fire over a medium-low heat for 5 minutes, then flip it over and brush the wings with marinade. Grill for another 5 minutes before flipping it back over and basting again. Repeat the grill-flip-baste process twice more, cooking the wings for about 20 minutes in total. Take them off the direct heat and set at the side of the grill to rest for 10 minutes before removing from the basket and serving.

To cook without a BBQ

Place the wings in a deep roasting tin and bake in a very hot oven (240°C/220°C fan/gas mark 9) for 10 minutes, then add the remaining marinade, mix well to baste, and return to the oven for another 10 minutes. Remove from the oven and turn all the wings over, basting them again with any juices formed in the bottom of the tin. Lift the wings carefully onto a rack and set it over the roasting tin. Return to the oven for a final 8–10 minutes to give the wings a deliciously sticky crust.

Chicken heart skewers

Makes 8 skewers (allow 2 per person)

Many people have never eaten heart, which is a shame as it is easy to cook and has a pleasant, subtle flavour. The heart is a muscle (of course) and benefits from quick cooking over a very high heat to avoid becoming tough or chewy. Strangely enough, these skewers tend to be a favourite with kids, although we are not sure whether they're more drawn by the idea or the flavour. Finding chicken hearts for sale can sometimes be tricky, especially in the UK, but if you ask your butcher nicely, I am sure they will set some aside. It is a part of the bird that tends to get thrown away, but really it should be celebrated.

500 g / 1 lb 2 oz chicken hearts

2 tbsp flaky sea salt

2 lt / 3 ½ pints very cold water

For the cooking

1 bunch of parsley (about 40 g / 1½ oz)

2 garlic cloves, peeled and minced

½ tsp hot paprika (or a pinch of cayenne pepper)

a sprinkle of flaky sea salt

Clean the hearts, removing any white membrane and trimming away visible veins. Mix the salt and water in a large bowl, add the cleaned hearts and leave to soak for 30 minutes to draw out any impurities.

Pick and chop the parsley, mix with the minced garlic and set aside until needed.

Tip the soaked hearts into a colander or sieve to drain, then pat them dry with kitchen paper. Thread five or six on each skewer. Stack the charcoal on your BBQ really high to get a good heat. Sear the hearts for 2 minutes on each side on a very hot grill, then dip each skewer in the parsley-garlic mixture before placing on a serving plate. Sprinkle with the salt and paprika (or cayenne) and serve immediately.

To cook without a BBQ

Use a lightly oiled, preheated griddle pan over a really high heat on your stove and cook just as you would on the fire (but without the skewers).

Spicy chicken liver skewers

Makes 8 liver skewers (allow 2 per person) and 2 vegetable skewers

Offal, especially liver, played a huge part in the meals cooked over fire that we encountered on our travels. Liver instantly takes on a whiff of smoke when cooked quickly over an open flame, and it chars lightly to great effect. It was rarely served on its own, usually appearing on a table laden with flatbreads, chopped raw onions and parsley (often mixed with sumac for a little lemony tang), and a salad of fresh local vegetables in a dressing of sorts: in Turkey, a drizzle of pomegranate molasses mixed with herbs and chilli; in Jordan, some cumin-laden lemon juice; and in Palestine and Israel, a generous drizzle of tahini.

1 kg / 2 lb 4 oz chicken livers

2 red onions, peeled

2 red chillies

For the marinade

1 tbsp ground cumin

1 tbsp sweet paprika

1 tbsp smoked paprika

1 tbsp *urfa* chilli flakes

½ tsp chilli flakes

1 tsp table salt

about 4 tbsp olive oil (just enough to bind everything)

Clean the livers by removing any white tissue or veins with a sharp knife, then place in a large bowl. Mix all the spices for the marinade together and add just enough oil to create a thick paste. Pour the paste over the livers, stir well to coat, then divide them between the eight skewers. Set the skewers on a tray in the fridge for about 15–20 minutes while you heat the BBQ. Quarter the red onions and thread the pieces on another two skewers along with the chillies.

Once the BBQ is roaring hot, place the onion skewers on the grill first and allow them to char for a couple of minutes before adding the liver skewers. Be careful as liver tends to spit a little. Grill for 2 minutes on each side, then serve with the charred onions and chillies.

To cook without a BBQ

Use a preheated griddle pan over a really high heat on your stove and cook just as you would on the fire, but without the skewers. Watch out for the dreaded splatters.

Lamb & Other Meats

When I was a child, lamb was a special occasion food. If we were going out to a restaurant, perhaps one or two of us might order lovely lamb chops as an extravagant treat, but we rarely cooked them at home other than to celebrate major religious holidays, particularly Passover, which occurs in spring. My mum would get together with some friends and neighbours to agree what meat to order, so that they could share the delivery costs. We had a great local supplier and he would arrange for beautiful (very expensive) cuts to be delivered.

Eventually, as we became more immersed in Israeli food culture, we understood that lamb was fundamental to local eating habits, with grill restaurants using every part of the animal to make shawarma, kofta, skewers of cubed meat, chops and (the most prized cut) little cubes of pure fat from the *alya*, the tail.

One year, when Passover happened to coincide with the Muslim festival of *Eid al-Fitr*, celebrating the end of Ramadan, my father walked in with a freshly butchered lamb carcass, a gift from a colleague. The house was sparkling clean, the table laid, and dinner already in the oven. My mum shrieked with dismay and sent my dad to the backyard to cut the meat up straight away, with strict instructions to have it safely in the freezer before any guests arrived. We happily feasted on those cuts for weeks to come.

You will find a few beef and pork recipes here, although not many, as you don't come across these meats as frequently in the Eastern Mediterranean. There isn't enough good grazing to rear cattle, so beef is usually imported and therefore expensive, and pork is only really available in Greece, as both Muslims and Jews have laws against its consumption. However, lamb is popular throughout the area, and this chapter is full of great, simple ways to prepare and cook it. Our menu always has at least one lamb dish on it, and we encourage you to eat it more often, since there is plenty of good, affordable lamb to be had in the UK.

That said, some of the best lamb dishes we have ever eaten were in southern Turkey; we strongly advise you to go and try them for yourself. Reared, butchered, prepared and cooked locally, in this lovely region of green fields, mountains, and cities full of delicious food, lamb reigns supreme.

LAMB & OTHER MEATS

Adana, Turkey: Adana kebabs, a near impossible recipe

On menus all over Turkey and throughout the world, wherever there's a Turkish community, you will see Adana kebab on offer. It is the golden standard of meat on a stick, and the cause of much controversy. What makes a kebab an Adana kebab? It's said to be a well-guarded recipe, with secret seasoning or a special meat-to-fat ratio. The whole thing is shrouded in mystery.

If you really want to know about grills and kebabs, you have to go to the source, to Adana. So we did, and we were lucky enough to be taken under the wing of Tayab. If Adana is the Hollywood of kebabs, then Tayab is Spielberg. Walking in Adana with him is like walking with the godfather – everyone comes out to shake hands and chat, every restaurant begs him to come in and try their cooking, but he is a discerning customer, and he's in a rush; he wants to show us this town, the best it has to offer. We go for a breakfast of grilled lamb's liver, a traditional breakfast here, as the delicate offal is only eaten in the morning, as close as possible to the time of slaughter. After that he takes us to the famous stone bridge and to the market, and from there to the Grand Mosque and the Madrasa, where artisans practise their calligraphy in the tranquil rose garden. Then out of town we go to see the Seyhan Dam, the beating heart of the entire region, channelling water to the heartlands and to the fields that make this one of the best growing regions in the world.

When we ask Tayab about Adana kebabs he offers to take us to his restaurant, where his chefs can teach us, no problem. We were expecting a bit more reticence, but Tayab shrugs – there is no mystery here, no special seasoning or secret spice. What makes it so good is the Adana lamb, which is second to none. As to the rest of the process, there are a few rules to follow, but certainly no secrets.

How to make Adana kebab, as taught to us by Tayab

The most important ingredient for an Adana kebab is lamb from the Adana region, those plump animals with really fatty tails you see on your drive from town (those tails and the fat in them are prized here). Any cut will do but you need a good amount of fat, about a fifth of the total quantity; if the cut is very lean you can supplement it with some tail fat. The next thing you'll need is a *zirh* (this is non-negotiable), the curved knife which every cook in Turkey swears by. They can be quite large, but for domestic use a small to medium-sized one will do. There's a local saying that the *zirh*, despite being quite intimidating to look at, is not a blade for war but a blade for joy. It is actually very easy to use and very effective.

First cut your meat into smallish pieces, as you would with a regular kitchen knife; then, holding the handle with one hand, place your other hand on the other side of the knife, very much minding your fingers, and start rocking the blade back and forth over the meat on the board, stopping every so often to retrieve any meat stuck to it, again minding your fingers. Continue until the meat is a coarse paste. This may take a while to achieve, certainly a lot longer than buying ready-minced meat, but it is crucial for the texture. The chefs who taught us were able to reduce hunks of meat to neat mince within seconds, and while we don't expect to reach that level of expertise in our lifetime, it certainly gets easier and faster with practice.

The seasoning is minimal – a bit of salt, black pepper and some red pepper flakes; nothing too spicy, as this is all about the flavour of the exquisite Adana lamb. Mix it very gently. You want to keep the texture loose as you shape the meat into a fist-sized patty. The skewering is an art in itself, and one that can be hard to master. You need a long, flat skewer. Hold it with one hand, pointing upwards, then use the other hand to wrap the patty gently around the top and squeeze it down between your thumb and forefinger, sliding down as you would on the frets of a guitar till it is evenly distributed all along the skewer. You need to be fast and confident and use just the right amount of pressure; too soft and it won't stick, too hard and the whole thing will break. It's quite simple to do actually. You just need to have confidence, which comes after a couple of hundred times of trying…

Now for the cooking: you need a shallow grill full of white-hot coals. The grill needs to be the width of your kebab (or rather your kebab needs to be no wider than your grill). Have a flatbread at hand – this is not only part of the dish but also a cooking utensil. Place your kebab on the grill, not too high above the coals, and let it colour for a minute or two, then turn it over, letting it sear on both sides. It'll start to sweat a bit as it releases liquids. These are too precious to be lost, and this is where your flatbread comes into play.

Remove the skewer from the heat and gently place it onto the bread, wrapping the entire kebab and swaddling it like a baby. Let the bread absorb all those beads of fat and juice, then unwrap it and return the kebab to the grill to finish cooking (keep the bread to one side as we are not done with it yet). Turn the meat until it's evenly cooked all the way through but not a minute longer. Tayab's chefs can judge by eye and spy the little tells – the look, the smell – but we check by gently poking it with our fingers, hoping for the best.

Now, remember that bread? Take the cooked kebab and place it onto the bread, fold it around just as you did before. Then place a hand on top of this bundle and, with a confident movement, pull the skewer out, leaving the meat inside. Some add grilled tomatoes to the bundle, or sliced onions and rocket, but you can have it just as it is: bread and expertly, carefully prepared meat. You will not find it lacking.

LAMB & OTHER MEATS

Honey & Smoke's Adana kebabs

Makes 6 long kebabs

The best way to make these is to mince the lamb with the vegetables and spices to integrate fully, but as a shortcut (or if you don't own a meat grinder), you can buy pre-minced lamb, purée the vegetables with the seasoning and knead everything together thoroughly to combine.

700 g / 1 lb 9 oz lamb shoulder meat (or 20% fat lamb mince)

1 red pepper, deseeded and sliced (about 150 g / 5¼ oz)

1 red chilli, halved, deseeded and sliced

2 onions, peeled and roughly diced (about 200 g / 7 oz)

5 garlic cloves, peeled

1 large bunch of parsley, leaves picked (about 40 g / 1½ oz)

2 tsp table salt

1 tsp baking powder

1 tbsp ground cumin

1 tbsp sweet paprika

½ tsp ground allspice (pimento)

vegetable oil for shaping

Mince the lamb shoulder meat together with all the other ingredients using a medium grinder attachment. Divide the mixture in two. Change the blade on the mincer to a fine grinder attachment and mince half the mixture again. Combine the medium and finely minced lamb mixtures and knead well to create a uniform texture.

Alternatively, if you have bought pre-minced lamb, use a food processor to blitz all the other ingredients together to a smooth purée, then combine with the lamb mince and knead well to form a homogenous mixture.

Divide the kebab mixture into six portions, each of roughly 190 g / 6¾ oz. Set six long, flat metal skewers next to you, along with a small bowl of vegetable oil.

You can either shape the kebabs directly onto the skewers in the traditional fashion, or roll the mixture into free-form log shapes to thread on the skewers. Whichever method you chose, rub a little oil every now and then on the hand you are using to shape the mixture, so that the mince doesn't stick. If you are forming them the traditional way, use your hand to shape the mixture around the skewers to make long, flattish kebabs (about 20 cm / 8 inches long), pressing your fingers and thumb in small pulses to compress the mince and make it stick. Place the kebabs in the fridge to chill for at least 20 minutes and up to 24 hours.

You want to BBQ these over medium-hot charcoal – nothing too violent – as you want the centre to cook through without the exterior burning. They will take about 15 minutes to cook fully, turning occasionally to get a good even colour all over.

To cook without a BBQ

Place the skewers in a roasting tin in a very hot oven (240°C/220°C fan/gas mark 9) for 16 minutes. Alternatively, forget the skewers and cook as long, flattish patties in a preheated griddle pan on your stove just as you would on the fire.

Lamb kofta / kebabs – 3 versions

Lamb kofta, or kebabs, are a staple of Turkish grilled food, and there are seemingly as many versions as there are days in the year. Nearly all are based on the same simple preparation: a combination of excellent lamb mince, salt and occasionally some spices. It is the foods that accompany the lamb on the skewer that really make the difference: seasonal fruit like loquats or quince, wet garlic, wild desert mushrooms, aubergines, courgettes… all of them delicious, all benefiting from a turn on the grill. We spice up our koftas a little more than is common in Turkey, more in line with Lebanese or Palestinian seasoning.

Loquat and lamb kofta

Makes 4 large skewers (allow at least one per person)

Loquats (also known as Japanese medlars or Chinese plums) can be tricky to track down, but they are worth finding in their short season for this very specifically spiced kofta. The golden plum-like fruit holds its shape so well on the grill and the warm flesh, with its tangy sweetness, works wonderfully with the lamb.

12 firm loquats

olive oil for brushing and shaping

For the kofta

600 g / 1 lb 5 oz minced lamb (about 20% fat)

1 tbsp ground coriander

1 tsp ground ginger

1 tsp ground cinnamon

½ tsp *biber* chilli flakes (or Allepo)

½ tsp baking powder

1 tbsp flaky sea salt

Combine the ingredients for the kofta and knead well to form a homogeneous mixture. Divide into 12 balls, each of about 50 g / 1¾ oz.

Cut around each loquat from tip to base and pull apart the two halves. Remove the seeds and brush the cut surfaces with olive oil.

Sandwich each kofta between two loquat halves, then thread three stuffed loquats onto each skewer.

Place on the BBQ and cook over a medium heat for about 6 minutes. Carefully turn the skewers over and grill for a further 6 minutes, until the fruit has charred a little. Brush with a little extra olive oil and set on the side of the grill where the heat is very low for 8–10 minutes before serving.

To cook without a BBQ

Use a preheated griddle pan on your stove and cook just as you would on the fire.

New season garlic and lamb kofta

Serves 4 (allow one kofta and one head of garlic per person)

This dish is all about the garlic; the lamb definitely plays second fiddle. You will need new season still-wet bulbs so that they can easily be skewered, and the moisture will protect them from burning on the grill. Serve with a whole load of flatbread or soft, squidgy bread rolls (like the ones on page 227) so that you can press the soft garlic out of the bulb onto the bread, then top with the lamb.

4 whole new season wet garlic bulbs

a sprinkling of sugar

juice of 2 lemons

For the kofta

250 g / 9 oz minced lamb (about 20% fat)

1 small onion, peeled and grated

1 tbsp *baharat* spice mix (see page 218)

1 tsp flaky sea salt

½ small bunch of parsley, leaves picked and finely chopped (about 20 g/ ¾ oz)

Combine the ingredients for the kofta and knead well to form a homogeneous mixture. Divide into 4 balls, each of about 90 g / 3¼ oz.

Alternating between garlic and meat, thread two bulbs (piercing them from root to tip) and two kofta onto each skewer. You will need two skewers for this.

Place on the BBQ and cook over a medium heat for about 3 minutes. Carefully rotate the skewers and grill for a further 3 minutes. Continue turning and grilling until the garlic has coloured slightly all over (about 12 minutes in total). Remove the skewers from the grill and carefully slide the lamb and garlic into a small pan. Sprinkle with a little sugar, add the lemon juice and cover with a lid. Place on the side of the grill over a medium-low heat to simmer for about 20 minutes, or until the garlic feels very soft when pressed.

Serve with lots of bread, allowing each person to figure out how best to squeeze the soft garlic out of the bulb to spread on the bread before topping with lemony lamb.

To cook without a BBQ

Place the skewers in a roasting tin in a very hot oven (240°C/220°C fan/gas mark 9) and cook for 14 minutes. Remove from the oven, pop the lamb and garlic in a small pan, add the lemon juice and sugar, cover and return to the oven. Reduce the heat to 200°C/180°C fan/gas mark 6 and cook for 20–25 minutes before serving.

LAMB & OTHER MEATS

Patlican kebabs – lamb and aubergine kebabs

Makes 4 large skewers (allow at least one per person)

The classic Turkish kebab. These are a staple throughout the year, but even more so during the month of Ramadan. When the sun goes down and people can break their day-long fast, grills are laid with dozens of these skewers, all cooking at once to produce a delicious dinner for hundreds of very hungry guests. We don't really know why these specific kebabs are so popular in Ramadan; possibly because aubergines are rather forgiving and don't dry out when cooked in bulk on the grill, or perhaps just because they're really tasty.

2 long black aubergines (use the longest, thinnest aubergines you can find)

olive oil for brushing

For the meat patties

600 g / 1 lb 5 oz minced fatty lamb (about 20% fat)

1 onion, peeled and grated

1 tsp sweet paprika

1 tbsp ground cumin

1 tsp ground allspice (pimento)

½ tsp baking powder

1 tbsp flaky sea salt

1 tbsp tomato purée

Combine all the ingredients for the patties and knead well to form a homogeneous mixture. Divide into 12 balls of about 60 g / 2 ¼ oz each.

Cut each aubergine into slices of about 4 cm / 1 ½ inches thick (depending on the size of your aubergines you may need to cut each slice in half again – you need to end up with 16 slices). Brush the cut surfaces with olive oil.

Thread four slices of aubergine and three meatballs alternately onto each skewer, starting and finishing with a slice of aubergine. Push to compress the meatballs between the pieces of aubergine as you go.

Place on the BBQ and cook on a medium heat for about 5 minutes, then rotate the skewers and leave for a further 5 minutes. Continue turning and grilling the kebabs until they are cooked all over and the aubergine starts to feel soft – this will take about 20 minutes. It is important to cook these on a medium-high grill to allow time for them to cook through without burning the exterior.

To cook without a BBQ

Place the skewers in a roasting tin in a very hot oven (240°C/220°C fan/gas mark 9) for 12 minutes. Turn them over and cook for another 12 minutes or until the aubergines are nice and soft.

Gaziantep, Turkey: Sheep country

Akhmed tells us that if you fly over Gaziantep early in the springtime, you will see the city in the middle of a sea of purple, pink and white as all the surrounding pistachio trees come into bloom. The cool winters, hot summers, abundance of water and plentiful sunshine makes this region ideal for what is a rather fussy tree. This southern Turkish town is the capital of pistachios. Everywhere you look there are nut vendors and *baklava* shops, and the streets in the old town centre are even paved with round pebbles that have a grey, green tinge and look a bit like – yes – pistachios.

Akhmed tells us that there's a saying in Turkey: when you come to Gaziantep, come hungry. We are in Orkide, his family restaurant, and as he walks us through their pastry shop, a pistachio emporium, he tells us that there are over 60 grades of pistachio here – purple, pink, green and pale yellow, each with their particular uses. He lifts a dome and unwraps a sweet for us, a type of macaroon made with the highest, rarest grade of pistachio. Its gentle flavour is so delicate that it is damaged by too much heat or exposure to sunlight, so it must be protected.

It's a weekend morning and the place is full. Everyone comes for the legendary breakfast here, and it's not long before we discover why: our table is soon filled with not-so-little dishes, too many to count, each one a delicious treasure – just-baked bread, yogurt you can stand a spoon up in, local raw honey, perfectly-made jam, cooked and fresh salads, dips, juicy olives. Hot dishes come from the kitchen – eggs poached in butter, liver cooked with red pepper – we groan with pleasure as Akhmed looks on approvingly. This is what weekend breakfasts used to be like when he was a child. A big family, they would all gather at his grandmother's house; everyone would bring something, and the meal was a mosaic of varied little bites. Just when we think we cannot possibly eat anything else, the *katmer* arrives. It is the centrepiece, the reason everyone comes here. You can see it being made in the window: an expert chef takes a ball of dough, rolls it thinly and flings it into the air, then bashes it on the counter to stretch till it is translucent. He spreads it with cream and an abundance of ground green pistachios, then the corners of the dough are folded in like an envelope and smeared with a generous lick of butter. Into the oven it goes, till the cream bubbles and the pastry is good and crisp. This then gets a wash of syrup and is placed on a special square stand, before being ceremoniously carried to the already-laden table. The combination of the produce of the land – the nuts, the cream, the protein-rich flour – and the skills of the people here makes this a truly special dish. More than a delicious mouthful, it is something from deep in the culture of this place.

Later that day we visited a few shops which straddle a little street corner in a residential part of Gaziantep: a bakery, greengrocer's, grill house and butcher's shop, all of them belonging to the same family. They own land out of town, around the villages of Van and Siirt, prime sheep country, and the butcher's shop is the urban outpost of their rural operation. While we were there a couple of the country cousins came in, still with tiny flecks of blood on their trousers from the day's slaughter. They kill 100 sheep a day, they told us, and the seven best come here, to Altun Et.

LAMB & OTHER MEATS

We watched, mesmerized, as the carcasses were broken down with surgical precision by the old Syrian butcher. He worked with great confidence and at incredible speed, and you got the feeling he could do this blindfolded. He started with the hind quarters: legs were broken down in minutes to the individual muscles, trimmed of veins, tendons, nerves and silver skin, leaving just pristine dark pink flesh, to be cut into *kuş başı*, little cubes the size of a bird's head, seasoned with a dash of garlic and local red pepper powder. Together with *taraklik*, the meat from the chops, this is the most prestigious and expensive grill meat. Cuts from the front of the animal are reserved for slow cooking, while larger muscles are cleaned and cut up with a *zirh*, the huge crescent knife used by butchers in the region to chop, not mince, meat. But there is something here for everyone: from expensive delicacies to items sold at a third of the price, like *kavurma*, chopped-up lung meat cooked with onion and spice.

The butcher's is where this little collection of businesses started. The grill house came next, then the bakery and the greengrocer's. All owned by the same family, they share a symbiotic existence. The butcher takes peppers and herbs from the greengrocer to chop into his kofta, and onions, quince and garlic to go into the *lahma* mix. The *lahma* is sent next door to the bakery to be spread on top of dough to make *lahmacun*; the bakery makes the bread to go to the kebab shops, and more. The locals also buy meat and vegetables to prepare at home, which they may then bring back to be cooked in the bakery's big wood-fired oven. Each tray is marked with a name: sister Gizi, sister Filiz. We saw one lady arrive with a bucket of local cheese, grated with onions, herbs and spices. She asked the bakers to roll it into dough pockets and bake it for her, which they did, their fingers moving so fast we could barely see what they were doing, before setting the little pockets on a paddle and sending them to the oven. As they came out, the bakery was filled with the most mouth-watering smell of fresh dough and melted cheese. We were offered one but had to decline. We had come hungry to Gaziantep, at least we thought we had, but the culinary riches of this town and its generosity filled us to the brim.

LAMB & OTHER MEATS

Tahini BBQ lamb chops with fresh plums and spiced plum sauce

A feast for 4–6

If you can, buy nicely trimmed lamb racks without too much of a fat cap, so that you don't need to worry about rendering fat off them before dividing into individual chops. Be forewarned, though: there will be a fair amount of smoke while cooking these, so they are best grilled outside. We use tahini in a few different versions of BBQ sauce, as the sesame paste lends itself so well to roasted meats, adding a rich nutty note. Here we include anchovies for a savoury touch and pomegranate molasses for sweetness. The accompanying plum sauce is like a chutney or Chinese plum sauce, with its sweet, sour and spicy flavours. It partners perfectly with these rich BBQ chops, and also works amazingly with a simple roast chicken or duck. The BBQ and plum sauces can either be made shortly before grilling the chops, or up to a couple of days in advance.

2 racks of lamb, divided into 12–14 single chops

100 g / 3½ oz baby red chard (or lamb's lettuce

4 plums, halved and stones removed)

For the tahini BBQ sauce

150 g / 5¼ oz tahini paste

1 clove of garlic, peeled and minced

2 salted anchovies, chopped

1 tsp *pul biber* chilli flakes (or Allepo)

2 tbsp pomegranate molasses

100 ml / 3½ fl oz water, plus more if needed

1 tsp flaky sea salt

For the spiced plum sauce

6 plums, cut into eighths and stones removed

50 g / 1¾ oz sugar

1 clove of garlic

1 whole dried chilli, cracked in half and seeds shaken out

1 tsp Szechuan pepper

1 bay leaf

3 tbsp pomegranate molasses

½ tsp flaky sea salt

1 tbsp red wine vinegar

Use a stick blender or a small food processor to blitz the BBQ sauce ingredients to a smooth, thick paste. You may need to add a little more water to reach the desired custard-like consistency, depending on the variety of tahini. You can use the BBQ sauce straight away or keep it in the fridge for a day or two until needed.

Put the plum wedges, sugar, garlic, spices, bay leaf and pomegranate molasses in a small frying pan, place over a high heat and bring to the boil. Cook for 5 minutes until the plums soften and start falling apart, then remove from the heat and stir in the salt and vinegar. You can use this straight away, or cool and store in the fridge for a few days.

When you are ready to cook, brush half of the BBQ sauce over the chops, coating both sides. You will need the rest of the BBQ sauce to brush on the chops as they grill. Place the chops one by one on the rack above a hot BBQ. Grill for 2 minutes, then turn them over and brush with some more sauce. Grill for another 2 minutes before turning them back over and basting again. Repeat the grill-turn-baste process until the chops have cooked for a total of 6 minutes on each side. Remove to a serving platter with the baby chard spread over it.

Pop the plum halves on the BBQ, cut-side down. Grill for a minute or so just to warm a little, then add to the platter with the chops. Serve with the plum sauce on the side.

To cook without a BBQ

Use a lightly oiled, preheated griddle pan on your stove and cook just as you would on the fire. But have your extractor fan on full blast, as it will get very smoky!

Grilled leg of lamb

Serves up to 10 as part of a feast (or fewer, with cold meat left over for sandwiches)

A whole leg of lamb produces a good amount of meat and should really be the centrepiece for a party, so invite some friends, make plenty of colourful salads to serve alongside, and carve this glazed lamb with panache. We usually serve this pink, but if you prefer it well done, please add about half an hour to the initial cooking time, before starting the glazing process.

4 tbsp olive oil

3 sprigs of rosemary, leaves picked and chopped

3 sprigs of thyme, leaves picked and chopped

1 tbsp flaky sea salt

½ tsp freshly ground black pepper

1 leg of lamb (about 2–2.5 kg / 4 ½–5½ lb)

For the glaze

100 ml / 3½ fl oz pomegranate molasses

1 tsp chilli flakes

1 tsp salt

2 tbsp olive oil

Mix the oil with the chopped herbs, salt and pepper, then rub all over the lamb. If possible, rest the lamb at room temperature for a couple of hours before cooking; if you don't have time, don't worry – it's fine to start grilling straight away. Mix the ingredients for the glaze together in a small bowl.

Build a fire and let it settle to warm embers. Place the lamb on the BBQ to sear all over, rotating it every 5–6 minutes so it colours evenly, turning it at least five times. This will take about 25–30 minutes in total. Move the leg to a cooler part of the BBQ and stand it up on its wide end (or suspend it from a hook so it is hanging very close to the fire, wide-end down). Brush with some of the glaze and leave to cook for 15 minutes. Glaze again and allow to cook for a further 15 minutes, then lay it back on its side on the BBQ. Brush the top side with glaze and cook for 4 minutes. Rotate it, brush with glaze again and leave for 4 more minutes. Repeat this rotate-glaze-cook process until the leg is caramelised all over, roughly 20–25 minutes in total. Remove from the grill to a tray and lightly cover with aluminium foil. Leave to rest for 15–20 minutes before carving at the table.

To cook without a BBQ

Lay the oil-rubbed lamb leg in a deep roasting tin and place in a very hot oven (220°C/200°C fan/gas mark 7) for 20 minutes to colour on one side. Flip it over and leave for a further 20 minutes to colour the other side. Remove from the oven, brush with some of the glaze, reduce the temperature to 200°C/180°C fan/gas mark 6 and return the lamb to roast for 15 minutes. Rotate, glaze again and roast for another 15 minutes. Rotate, brush with glaze one more time and cook for a final 15 minutes. Turn the oven off but leave the leg in there to rest for 15–20 minutes before carving.

LAMB & OTHER MEATS

Crisp lamb on creamy hummus

Serves 4 as a main

Meat-topped hummus is the dish I missed the most as a teenager. I had decided at the age of 10 to become a vegetarian, not because I didn't enjoy the flavour of meat, but for the sake of the poor animals and, I suppose, for a bit of a challenge. It took me 10 years and the decision to become a chef before I started eating meat again. This meant that all through my teenage years I would watch the rest of my family devouring one of my favourite dishes, meat-topped hummus, while I would eat plain hummus, mushroom-topped hummus, tahini-topped hummus... you get the drift. Hummus can be topped with countless other foods and I love them all, but this crispy lamb may just be The One.

For the lamb

1 lamb breast on the bone, about 1.5 kg / 3 lb 5 oz
1 tbsp table salt
1 tbsp cumin seeds
1 tsp black peppercorns
2 onions, quartered
1 lt / 1¾ pints water

For the hummus

200 g / 7 oz dried chickpeas, soaked overnight in plenty of water so they double in volume
1 tsp bicarbonate of soda
1 clove of garlic, peeled
1 tsp table salt
250 g / 9 oz tahini paste
½ tsp ground cumin
2 tbsp lemon juice

To serve

a few sprigs of parsley, chopped (about 10 g / ⅓ oz)
1 tsp *biber* chilli flakes (or Allepo)

Rub the lamb all over with the salt, cumin seeds and peppercorns, and set in the fridge for about 2 hours. Place in a braising pan and add the onions and the water. Bring to the boil, then cover with a lid, reduce the heat to low, and simmer slowly for about 1½ hours.

While the lamb is in the fridge, or while it is simmering, prepare the hummus. Drain the soaked chickpeas, place in a large pan and cover with plenty of fresh cold water. Bring to the boil and skim off the foam that forms. Allow to boil for 5 minutes, then skim again.

Add the bicarbonate of soda and mix well – the whole thing will bubble up like a volcano. Skim it thoroughly, then cook at a steady simmer for about 30–40 minutes, skimming regularly, until the chickpeas soften entirely. By this time the foam should be really thick and yellow. Pull a couple of chickpeas out and try them; they should melt in your mouth without any resistance.

Remove the pan from the heat and drain the chickpeas into a colander sitting over a bowl, as you want to retain the cooking liquid. The drained weight should be about 600 g / 1 lb 5 oz. It is important to prepare the hummus while everything is still hot, to achieve a silky texture. Pour 250 ml / 8¾ fl oz of the retained cooking liquid over the chickpeas (either in a food processor or in the bowl if you are using a stick blender). Add the garlic clove and blitz until really smooth. It will look a little like a chickpea soup at this stage but don't worry! Add the rest of the hummus ingredients and continue blitzing until well combined. Cover the surface directly with cling film, to avoid a skin developing. It will still look runny, but will thicken as it cools; you may even need to add a touch of water to loosen it when it is cold.

Lift the lamb out of the cooking water, retaining a few spoonfuls for serving. The meat should feel soft and pull away from the bones easily. Carefully lift onto a hot grill to char for about 10 minutes. Turn it over to char the other side for 10 minutes too, then remove to a chopping board. Use two forks to pull the meat apart, as if shredding crispy duck.

Spread the hummus on a serving platter, top with the lamb and drizzle with the reserved lamb cooking liquid. Sprinkle with the chopped parsley and chilli flakes, and serve with plenty of pitta.

To cook without a BBQ

Use a preheated griddle pan on your stove to crisp the outside of the poached lamb just as you would on the fire. Alternatively, shred the meat after removing from the cooking liquid, then fry in a heavy-bottomed frying pan until crispy (no need to add any oil).

Thessaloniki, Greece: *Antikristo*

The restaurant Parasties is set in an old villa in a well-heeled part of town. The name is short for *para estia*, which means 'by the hearth', and the hearth is indeed the first thing you see as you walk into the place. The restaurant has a counter facing a simple fire pit which runs the length of the entire back wall, with racks that are propped up on breeze blocks, which serve to separate the grill into compartments with varying levels of heat. Two cooks in jaunty, colourful bonnets are working the grill, their hands like those of concert pianists, gliding across the bars, moving skewers and cuts of meat, shifting pots and pans, turning around to the counter to slice, dress, plate or garnish, then turning back to the grill at exactly the right moment before the meat dries out or before the pan boils over. High above the grill, right under the extractor hood, are quarters of lamb on metal crosses, the dish this place is famous for.

We take a table at the back, in a glasshouse that has water flowing over its roof for some reason, maybe to keep it clean, or cool. Whatever the reason, the effect is quite soothing, like being by the beach. We want to order everything. There's a big table sitting next to us which has just received a huge, puffy frittata that we saw the chefs cooking on the grill. We sadly give it a miss, but what we do order doesn't disappoint. The salad comes in a ceramic trough the size of a kitchen sink ; now we understand why our waiter tried to get us to order something else. The courgette fritters turn out to be little deep-fried pies with a cheese and courgette stuffing. Slices of smoked, spice-rubbed pork neck are served with a kind of aubergine and pepper relish, sweet and smoky from the grill.

The main event is that lamb which we saw suspended high above the grill. This is *antikristo*. If, like us, you thought the name had biblical origins – the lamb, the cross, the hellish flames – then, like us, you'd be wrong. The literal translation is 'facing the flames', a succinct description of this famous Cretan dish. Lambs are quartered, salted, skewered and placed facing the flames to cook slowly in the gentle, indirect heat, which allows the muscles to soften and fat to render.

The cooks pull down a quarter of lamb on its cross and chop a portion for us. The slow cooking and wood smoke somehow concentrate the flavour, making it taste more meaty, more intense, each bite highlighting the slightly different qualities of each muscle.

This is traditionally a dish cooked by men. They say it can be traced back to the time of Homer, when soldiers in ancient Crete used to spear the lamb on their swords. In later centuries, shepherds would build a fire in a pit and place the meat in a circle around it to be energy efficient and make the most of the heat. This is the most rudimentary form of cooking, pared down to its bare elements – meat, fire, stick – but sitting here in Parasties, it tastes like the height of sophistication.

Antikristo – smoked and charred lamb shoulder

Serves 6–8 hungry guests

You will need two long metal skewers for this dish, unless you have a built-in rotisserie attachment for your BBQ. The skewers will provide a sturdy cross-shaped frame for the lamb, holding it in place while it cooks and smokes over the fire. You can ask any butcher to de-bone the shoulder for you. Then you just need a good bit of butcher's twine or cooking string to tie it in a roll after seasoning.

1 de-boned lamb shoulder, about 1.8 kg / 4 lb

For the seasoning

2 tbsp dried Greek oregano

1 clove of garlic, peeled and minced

1 tbsp whole coriander seeds, roughly crushed

zest of 1 lemon

2 tbsp flaky sea salt

½ tsp freshly ground black pepper

Mix the seasoning ingredients together and rub all over the meat. Roughly roll the lamb into a log-shape and tie with some butcher's twine or kitchen string to form a large rectangle. It doesn't need to be perfect, so don't spend hours trying to get it straight. Thread one of the large metal skewers diagonally through from the top left corner to bottom right corner of the rectangle, and the second skewer from the top right corner to the bottom left corner, to form a cross onto which the lamb is securely threaded. Wrap and place in the fridge for a couple of hours or, even better, overnight.

Build a fire stack with lots of wood and paper, and place the lamb on a rack just above the centre of the stack. Cover the meat with a large metal bowl or saucepan, then light the fire so that when the smoke wafts up, it will be collected around the lamb and impart some of its flavour and smokiness to the meat. Leave to smoke for 6 minutes, then remove the cover and flip the lamb over. Re-cover and allow 6 more minutes to smoke the other side. Remove the cover again, but this time pop the lamb into it and set it aside until you have lovely hot embers glowing.

Place the lamb back on the rack over the hot coals and sear for 10 minutes on each side until the meat chars a little and crisps up. Now you want to continue cooking the lamb, but away from direct heat. This is where the crossed skewers help. Prop the lamb upright on the skewers so it is standing above the fire, but not directly touching it (or suspend it from a rotisserie attachment, if you have one). After half an hour, turn the lamb the other way up, standing the other two skewers in the fire, and leave to cook for a further 30 minutes. Remove to the side of the grill where the heat is low to cook for a final 30 minutes, then rest for at least 15 minutes before slicing thinly.

To cook without a BBQ

Place in a deep roasting tin and cook in a very hot oven (240°C/220°C fan/gas mark 9) for 25 minutes. Reduce the heat to 200°C/180°C fan/gas mark 6 and roast for another 30 minutes. Pour a cup of water over the lamb to baste the shoulder, then cover the roasting tin with aluminium foil or a fitting lid and roast for another hour. Reduce the heat once more, this time to 180°C/160°C fan/gas mark 4, and baste the lamb with the juices in the bottom of the tin. You can add a little extra water if it seems dry – the liquid level should be around a quarter of the way up, no more. Cover again and leave to roast for a final hour before serving.

Beer-braised smoky pork ribs

Serves 4–6 as part of a meal

2 racks of baby back pork ribs (each about 900 g / 32 oz)

For the salt rub

2 garlic cloves

8 sage leaves

6 sprigs of thyme, leaves picked

zest of 1 lemon

3 tbsp flaky sea salt or *sel gris*

½ tsp freshly ground black pepper

For braising

250 ml / 8¾ fl oz dark beer of your choice

250 ml / 8¾ fl oz water

2 shallots or 1 onion, unpeeled and halved

4 garlic cloves, unpeeled

6–8 thyme sprigs

Use a pestle and mortar to roughly crush all the salt rub ingredients together to a rough sand consistency. Sprinkle all over the ribs, wrap and place in the fridge for at least 4 hours and up to 24 hours.

Prepare a stack with lots of wood and paper, so it will be very smoky once lit. Remove the ribs from the fridge and dab dry with paper towels. Set them on the grill and light the stack. Let the smoke start billowing up, then place an upturned roasting tin over the ribs to collect the smoke around the meat. Leave for about 10 minutes, then lift the ribs off the grill and pop them in the tin that was covering them.

Alternatively use a home-made smoker (see page 239) to smoke the ribs for about 10 minutes, then pop them in a large roasting tin.

Add the braising ingredients to the ribs, cover the tin with aluminium foil or a fitting lid, and set at the side of the BBQ while the fire subsides into lovely hot embers. Place the tray over the heat to braise for about 1½ hours, uncovering every 20 minutes

or so to baste and check the liquid level – it should be about halfway up the ribs. Add a little kindling to the fire every now and then, just to keep it ticking along.

Check the ribs are done by pulling at the end of a bone; it should just start to come away from the meat. You can serve these straight away or, if you prefer a few crispy bits, stoke the fire up to a really high heat, then carefully lift the ribs from the liquid and pop them directly on the grill to caramelize for 5 minutes on each side before serving.

To cook without a BBQ

You can smoke the ribs in a simple home-made smoker and then braise in the oven at 190°C/170°C fan/gas mark 5 to great effect. Give them a final blast of heat for 5 minutes each side in a hot griddle pan or under the grill before serving.

Smoked beef short ribs with black pepper and orange

Enough for 4–6

For best results, you should start preparing this a day in advance, so that the salt rub can penetrate the meat overnight to give it a really great flavour. This is a rich, fatty and satisfying dish that only needs a fresh salad on the side to make a whole meal.

850 g–1 kg / 30–35 oz beef short ribs (also known as Jacob's ladder)

For the salt rub

1 tbsp coarse sea salt (ideally coarse *sel gris*, if you have it)

1 tbsp black peppercorns

1 tbsp whole coriander seeds

zest of 1 orange

For smoking

1 tbsp coriander seeds

a handful of wood chips

1 tbsp sugar

Contents of 1 tea bag or 1 heaped tsp dried tea leaves

For slow-cooking

100 ml / 3½ fl oz fresh orange juice

100 ml / 3½ fl oz water

1 large onion, unpeeled

For the rub, use a pestle and mortar to roughly crush the salt, peppercorns and coriander seeds, then stir in the orange zest. Set aside one tablespoon of the mixture to serve and rub the rest all over the meat. Wrap the beef and place in the fridge overnight, or for at least 6 hours, to dry-brine.

Place the coriander seeds, wood chips and sugar in the base of a deep tray and scatter the tea leaves over them. Place the beef on a wire rack or perforated tray that can fit in the deep tray. Light the wood chips with a couple of lit coals or a blow torch, place the beef on its tray or rack above the smouldering wood and cover securely with foil or a well-fitting lid to avoid any smoke escaping. Leave to smoke for 20 minutes then uncover and remove the beef. Discard the burning matter and transfer the meat directly to the bottom of the tray.

Add the orange juice, water and whole onion to the tray, cover well, and place on a low heat on the BBQ or in the oven at 170°C/150°C fan/gas mark 3–4. Cook for 2–3 hours, basting every 30 minutes and adding a little water to the tray if it dries out too much, until the beef is fully cooked and comes away from the bone very easily.

Carefully lift the short ribs from the tray and place directly on the BBQ for about 10–12 minutes to give them a final char and blast of smoke, then sprinkle with the retained tablespoon of salt rub mixture and serve straight away.

To cook without a BBQ

Smoke the ribs as above and then braise in a covered pan in the oven at 170°C/150°C fan/gas mark 3–4 for about 2½ hours, basting every half an hour, until the meat is soft. Remove the lid, increase the temperature to 220°C/200°C fan/gas mark 7 and give the ribs a final blast for 10–12 minutes before serving.

LAMB & OTHER MEATS

Pork chops with spiced butter

A quick dinner for 2

This invariably ends up being a staple dinner when we are on holiday. We buy a couple of chops and a local spice mix, light a small BBQ in the garden and cook this just for the two of us.

2 large potatoes

2 large pork chops on the bone

juice of 1 lemon

For the spiced butter

50 g / 1¾ oz butter (or ghee)

1 tsp sweet paprika

1 tsp ground coriander

½ tsp ground allspice (pimento)

a pinch of freshly ground black pepper

1 tsp dried oregano

1 tbsp olive oil

zest of 1 lemon

1 garlic clove, peeled and crushed

½ tsp salt

Build a BBQ and let it settle to nice hot embers. Wrap the potatoes in foil and pop them in the coals about 45 minutes before you want to eat.

Melt the butter in a small pan and stir in the spices, oregano, olive oil, lemon zest, garlic and salt. Remove from the heat and leave to infuse for 5 minutes.

Brush the chops on one side with the spiced butter and lay them buttered-side down on the BBQ. Grill for 5 minutes, brushing butter on the top (previously unbuttered) side of the chops as they cook. Flip them over to grill for 5 minutes on the other side, again basting the top side with butter. Remove to a plate.

Pull the softened potatoes from the embers and leave to cool for a few minutes until you can easily unwrap them. Slit them down the middle and pour the rest of the seasoned butter over them. Serve with the chops and drizzle the lemon juice all over.

To cook without a BBQ

Bake the potatoes in a hot oven (220°C/200°C fan/gas mark 7) for 45–60 minutes until soft. Use a preheated griddle pan on your stove and cook the chops just as you would on the fire.

Ribeye steak with smoky pepper salad

To serve 4 as part of a meal

We grilled the steak pictured here for a large gathering after a day at the beach. The children with us were starving and kept sneaking little fingers into salad bowls and grabbing whatever had just been cooked. We told them that they needed to be patient, since a good steak on the bone takes time to grill, but that it would be worth the wait. Surprisingly, they did wait patiently for us to cook it… and then we (adults) really regretted advising them to do so, as they devoured the entire steak in minutes.

1 large ribeye steak on the bone
(650–750 g / 23–26 oz)

olive oil for brushing

flaky sea salt

freshly ground black pepper

For the smoky pepper salad

2 large, long Romano peppers

1 red chilli

1 small bunch of parsley, leaves picked and chopped

3 sprigs of fresh tarragon, leaves picked and chopped

1 clove of garlic

4 spring onions, finely chopped

flaky sea salt

freshly ground black pepper

zest and flesh of 1 lime

2 tbsp red wine vinegar

3 tbsp olive oil

Once your fire is really hot, place the peppers and chilli on the grill to char all over until they are blackened, soft and deeply smoky. Remove to a small bowl, cover and leave to steam a little, so that you can easily peel them.

While you are waiting for the peppers and chilli to char, mix the herbs with the garlic, spring onions, salt, pepper and lime zest. Peel the lime and dice the flesh into little cubes. Peel the peppers and chilli, remove the seeds and cut the flesh into thin strips. Add the lime flesh, peppers and chilli to the herb mixture, and pour in the vinegar and oil. Stir well, taste to check the seasoning and adjust as necessary.

Brush the steak lightly with olive oil and season well all over with salt and pepper. Place on a medium grill for 5 minutes, so that the outside has time to caramelize beautifully without overcooking. Flip the steaks over to cook for 5 minutes on the other side. Repeat this process to cook for a total of 10 minutes on each side. Remove to a platter and loosely cover with aluminium foil to rest without cooling too much – about 10 minutes should be perfect. Top with the smoky pepper salad and serve.

To cook without a BBQ

You can char the peppers and chilli directly on a gas hob or under the grill. Caramelize the beef in a very large ovenproof frying pan for about 5 minutes on each side, then pop in the oven to roast for 12 minutes at 200°C/180°C fan/gas mark 6. Allow to rest before serving, as above. You won't have the delicious smokiness that cooking over fire gives you, but you can compensate by adding a really large knob of butter to the frying pan and/or seasoning with smoked salt rather than regular.

Bread & Unmissables

The magic that makes a meal complete

This chapter is the last in the book, but contains some of the most important recipes.

It starts with our favourite spice blends – the holy trinity of sweet spice, baharat and ras el hanout – that form the basis of our little kitchen empire. We make our own blends in bulk to use daily in the restaurants, as well as to sell in Honey & Spice.

Try to source good-quality, fresh, whole spices at a proper grocer's shop; you will be able to tell by the colour and smell whether the spices are fresh; there should be no mustiness, just a zingy aroma. Better still, if you go travelling in the Middle East, ask local people to direct you to the best place to buy spices; there are speciality shops dotted all over the region. The prices tend to be reasonable and the quality is far superior to anything you could buy in a tiny supermarket jar. Roast and grind the spices as and when you need them for results that are well worth the extra work.

After the spices come a few recipes for bread, a staple in meals all around the Mediterranean. You will find a basic flatbread along with some variations, all of which are best grilled over the fire, plus a couple of fuller, softer-textured, more complex breads that will make almost any meal into a celebration.

We finish with just two desserts to round off the party. This is a book about cooking over fire and our travels researching it, and puddings didn't often feature. That said, we are Honey & Co, so we always end on a sweet note.

211

Amman, Jordan: Sweet note

Driving back to Amman after a day trekking in the hills near Ajloun in northern Jordan, we stopped for fuel and to stretch our legs. At the kiosk there was a small coal pit where strong cardamom coffee was being brewed and *knafe* was being cooked, a savoury-sweet snack of cheese and *kadaif* pastry drenched in flower-scented syrup, which needs to be eaten fresh and hot, so the cheese is melting and the pastry crisp. In Jordan, it always seems to be a good moment to eat *knafe*. An evening with friends in downtown Amman is not complete without a stop at Habiba, possibly the best sweet shop in the Middle East. Whenever there is something to celebrate – an engagement, a birth or just a family gathering – there will be a guy there from the local pastry shop to make *knafe*. Or just a joyous little moment like this, at a wonky metal table by a petrol station at the side of the road, the bitter coffee and sweet dessert making a perfect afternoon pick-me-up.

Back at our hotel in Amman, grubby and dusty from our travels, we stood in stark contrast to the rest of the scene in the lobby: men smelling of fine cologne, dressed in sharp suits, silk ties and luxury watches, women in colourful sparkling ball gowns, with immaculate make-up and elaborate hair, all guests arriving for a society wedding. They descended the stairs to the pool, while the rest of us watched. There was a crowd at the bottom of the steps, and

music. Tambourines and big drums beat fast, shrill wind instruments played a jaunty tune and men huddled close together, singing, dancing and waving alarmingly big swords over their heads. The women across from them clapped and swayed shoulder to shoulder, the light and movement making them look like a gently-revolving, multi-coloured glitter ball. Every new guest joined this happy throng. There was more singing, more drums, more swords, and everybody smoked.

We watched, thrilled, and really wanted to join the party. Maybe this elegant crowd would forgive our grubbiness because we are foreigners and cute. We thought a suited guy was going to invite us, but instead he asked us to move aside for the bride and groom. They were as beautiful as any young couple in a society wedding should be. The crowd of around 500 people roared as the couple appeared at the top of the stairs and it was like a rock concert; the music became louder, faster, happier, the singing almost shouting, the dancing almost jumping. The bride and groom held their hands high to face their crowd, dancing until the banisters lit up with a flash of fireworks. Ecstasy. They took the stairs one at a time, the crowd cheering each descent, and when they finally reached the floor, they were engulfed in song and dance, well-wishes and good cheer. They walked around the pool, from which occasional bursts

of fireworks erupted. We watched this procession, really wanting to play a part somehow, wishing we could get married again, like this.

On the way to our room we saw the chefs with trolleys of desserts for the buffet. They were a lot friendlier to us than the wedding guests, and when we told them we were also chefs, they showed us their set-up: a buffet that seemed to last for ever with endless salads and breads, and mounds of *mansaf*, Jordan's national dish. There was a shawarma stand and a grill heating up, with trays and trays of skewered, marinated meat ready to go. Someone gave us stuffed vine leaves to try, herby and lemon-sharp; someone else came over with fresh falafel and a plate of starters. They were all so proud of their cooking and a lot calmer than we would have been if we were about to feed 500 people. The pastry brigade arrived to set up the dessert table with a mountain of sweets, a mad mash-up of East and West: *baklava* and profiteroles; New York cheesecakes and *halawet el jibn*, a Jordanian cheese dessert; creamy chocolate mousses and crisp Syrian fennel biscuits. We counted at least 30 different desserts, and the pastry chef would have had us try each one. If only! Just as they rolled in a two-metre high, seven-tiered wedding cake, we asked the pastry chef if he thought he had made enough sweets. "No," he said, "we've got the *knafe* guy coming later."

BREAD & UNMISSABLES

Sweet spice mix

We use this not only for cakes and baked goods but also for savoury preparations that require a lighter touch. It is also a core element in our baharat spice mix.

10 cardamom pods

6 cloves

½ nutmeg

1 tsp whole fennel seeds

2 tsp whole *mahleb* seeds

3 tsp ground ginger

4 tsp ground cinnamon

Heat your oven to 190°C/170°C fan/gas mark 5. Roast the cardamom pods, cloves and nutmeg on a baking tray for 5 minutes, then add the fennel and *mahleb*, and roast for another 5 minutes. Remove from the oven and allow to cool completely before grinding and mixing with the pre-ground ginger and cinnamon. Store in a dry, airtight container, ideally in the freezer. This will keep for up to 6 months, but I always think you should try to use it within 2 months to get the flavour at its best.

Baharat (aka Sarit) spice mix

We call this Sarit spice because, like its namesake, it is the backbone of everything we make. It is the primary spice mix we use for seasoning food throughout the company and at home. It takes a little time to prepare, so it is worth making a large batch and storing whatever you are not using in the freezer to keep fresh. If you can't be bothered to make it yourself, we sell it online and in our shops. Alternatively, you could use a ready-made mix from a supermarket or a local grocer's; simply ask for their baharat. It won't be the same as ours, but it should still be tasty.

1 dried chilli

3 tsp coriander seeds

4 tsp cumin seeds

2 tsp ground pimento

1 tsp white pepper

½ tsp ground turmeric

2 tsp sweet spice mix (see left)

Heat your oven to 190°C/170°C fan/gas mark 5. Crack the chilli open and shake out the seeds. Place the deseeded chilli on a baking tray with the coriander and cumin seeds and roast for 6 minutes.

Remove from the oven and allow to cool entirely on the tray. Crumble the chilli between your fingers, then grind to a powder with the roasted seeds. Mix with the other spices and store in a dry, airtight container, ideally in the freezer. This will keep for up to 6 months, but I always think you should try to use it within 2 months to get the flavour at its best.

Ras el hanout spice mix

There are as many versions of this spice mix as there are spice shops in the Middle East. The literal translation of *ras el hanout* is 'head of the shop', meaning the best the shop has to offer, and can contain up to twenty different spices. This is our version, which you can either make yourself or buy ready-made from us (online or at our shops) if you prefer.

60 g / 2¼ oz cumin seeds

60 g / 2¼ oz coriander seeds

90 g / 3¼ oz fenugreek seeds

3 whole cloves

2 dried Persian limes

30 g / 1 oz whole cardamom pods

20 g / ¾ oz dried rose petals

20 g / ¾ oz curry leaves

1 tsp cayenne pepper

1 tbsp ground white pepper

1 tbsp ground turmeric

1 tbsp ground cinnamon

1 tbsp *amchoor* (mango powder)

1 tbsp sweet paprika

Heat your oven to 190°C/170°C fan/gas mark 5. Place the cumin, coriander, fenugreek, cloves, dried limes and cardamom pods on a baking tray. Roast for 5 minutes, then add the rose petals and curry leaves and roast for another 3 minutes.

Remove from the oven and cool before using a spice grinder to grind to a powder. Mix with the pre-ground spices. Store in a dry, airtight container, ideally in the freezer. This will keep for up to 6 months, but I always think you should try to use it within 2 months to get the flavour at its best.

Griddle bread – base recipe and 2 variations

Makes 14 side-plate sized breads, or 7 large wraps that can easily contain a kebab

We have written in previous books about making griddled flatbreads. They come in many different varieties and play a big part in meals throughout the Middle East. This base recipe is lots of fun to make and can be used as a blank canvas for variations of your own.

As kids we used to cook them over campfires, on upturned woks or metal sheets. They occasionally contained more sand than anything else, but we were still excited to produce something that smelled so good and took only minutes to prepare. If doing this in the 'wild' (i.e. on a camping trip) on a hot weekend, you can omit the yeast and simply mix the rest of the ingredients together the evening before you intend to cook. Leave the mixture covered with a cloth until you are ready to shape the dough, as the warm weather and the wild yeasts in the air should be enough. However, if you are preparing dough to cook on the BBQ the same day, you'll need the yeast to get things going.

For the base dough

500 g / 1 lb 2 oz strong bread flour (actually plain flour works well too)	
1 tsp dried yeast	
2 tsp salt	
1 tsp sugar	
250–300 ml / 8¾– 10½ fl oz warm water	
2 tbsp vegetable oil	

You can make this dough by hand or use an electric mixer with a dough hook. Combine the flour with the yeast, salt and sugar, then add enough of the warm water to bind, mixing as you go until all the flour comes away from the sides of the bowl and you have a ball of dough. The amount of water needed will depend on the flour and the weather, so start with the smaller quantity and add more as required. Pour in the oil and knead vigorously for about 6–8 minutes to create a smooth, supple dough. Cover and rest for about an hour.

Plain griddle bread
Makes 14 side-plate sized breads

1 portion of base dough (see above)	
4 tbsp vegetable oil	

Divide the dough into 14 pieces, each about 60 g / 2¼ oz, and roll into balls. Pour the oil onto a tray and roll the dough balls in it to coat. Leave on the tray to rest for 30 minutes. Press each dough ball down on the work surface with your palm so it forms a thin round of about 15 cm / 6 inches in diameter. Lift the rounds carefully and place directly on a hot rack on the BBQ. Grill for about a minute until the dough loses its oily shine, then use tongs to carefully peel off and turn them over. Cook the other side for 30 seconds before removing. You can eat these immediately or (if you are serving them later) cover well or keep in an airtight container until needed.

BREAD & UNMISSABLES

Sumac, oregano and black pepper griddle bread

Makes 14 side-plate sized breads

1 portion of base dough (see recipe on page 220)

2 tsp sumac

4 tsp dried oregano

1 tsp freshly ground black pepper

4 tbsp olive oil

Add all spices to the base dough and knead well to work them through.

Divide the dough into 14 pieces, each about 60 g / 2¼ oz, and roll into balls. Pour the oil onto a tray and roll the dough balls in it to coat. Leave on the tray to rest for 30 minutes. Press each dough ball down on the work surface with your palm so it forms a thin round of about 15 cm / 6 inches in diameter. Lift the rounds carefully and place directly on a hot rack on the BBQ. Grill for about a minute until the dough loses its oily shine, then use tongs to carefully peel off and turn them over. Cook the other side for 30 seconds before removing. You can eat these immediately or (if you are serving them later) cover well or keep in an airtight container until needed.

Herby cheese-filled griddle bread

Makes 6 stuffed flatbreads (great as a light meal or on their own)

1 portion of base dough (see recipe on page 220)

extra flour for dusting

100 g / 3½ oz baby spinach, washed and roughly chopped

1 bunch of dill, fronds picked and chopped (20 g / ¾ oz)

1 bunch of parsley, leaves picked and chopped (30 g / 1 oz)

5 spring onions, finely chopped

5 sprigs of thyme, leaves picked

1 tsp flaky sea salt

a good sprinkling of freshly ground black pepper

120 g / 4¼ oz strong dry sheep's cheese, like *kashkaval* or Pecorino

Divide the base dough into 6 pieces, each about 140 g / 5 oz, and roll into balls. Dust the work surface with a little flour and use a rolling pin to flatten each ball out to a rough round of about 20 cm / 8 inches in diameter.

Mix the rest of the ingredients together in a bowl, then divide between the dough rounds, heaping the filling in the middle and leaving a 5 cm / 2 inch rim clear around the edges. Brush the dough rim with a little water and fold the round in half so that the filling is encased (rather like a calzone pizza). Use a fork to press the edges of the dough together to seal. Carefully place the filled rounds on a medium-hot rack on the BBQ, or in a large, lightly oiled frying pan that has been heated in advance. Grill (or pan-fry) for 4 minutes, then flip very carefully and cook for another 4 minutes on the other side. Serve warm.

Pebble bread

Makes 6 large breads

The name of this bread comes from how it is cooked, which – as you may have guessed – is on hot pebbles. The most common method is to line the base of a wood-burning oven with large, smooth pebbles (you can put them in a tray so they are easier to insert and remove from the oven) and leave them to heat up with the fire before popping the dough on top. If you are lucky enough to be using such an oven, you simply close the hatch to keep heat in and leave the bread to bake. If you are making this on a BBQ or fire, you will need to create a makeshift oven using an upturned wok or large metal bowl over a cast-iron tray or pan containing the stones. The pebbles give the bread little crisp edges and crusts, and create a funky-looking flat loaf, but be very careful when removing the bread, in case any have embedded themselves in the dough, as they will be very hot.

350–400 ml / 12¼–14 fl oz cold water

20 g / ¾ oz fresh yeast

1 tsp sugar

500 g / 1 lb 2 oz strong bread flour, plus extra for shaping

1 tsp flaky sea salt, plus extra for finishing

1 tsp whole fennel seeds

1 tbsp dried rosemary

60 ml / 2¼ fl oz olive oil, plus extra for finishing

Place the water, yeast, sugar and flour in this order in the bowl of an electric mixer with a hook attachment and knead on a low speed for 2 minutes. Add the salt, fennel seeds and rosemary and increase the speed to medium. Drizzle in the olive oil and continue kneading on a medium speed for 3 minutes until you have a smooth dough. Increase the speed to full and knead for a final 5 minutes. The dough should now be shiny and stretchy. Cover the bowl and leave to rest for 30 minutes.

Sprinkle some flour on your work surface and turn the dough out. Divide into 6 pieces (each about 160 g / 5¾ oz) and roll into balls. Sprinkle with a little more flour and rest for a further 30 minutes.

While the dough is resting, get your wood-burning oven or BBQ nice and hot. Place a large cast-iron tray (or pan) lined with washed pebbles inside the oven or on the fire, so that the pebbles have plenty of time to heat through. Check them by splashing with a bit of water – it should fizzle and steam off immediately (as it would in a sauna).

Press each dough ball down to flatten into a large pebble-shape, about 2–3 cm / ¾–1¼ inches thick. You can use a rolling pin if you prefer, but it is easy enough to do it with your palms. Carefully place the flattened dough directly on the hot stones. You may have to bake this bread in batches, depending on the size of your tray. Close the oven or place an upturned wok or large metal bowl over the pebble tray and leave the bread to bake for 6–8 minutes until golden. Use tongs to remove to a rack on the side. Brush with a little olive oil and sprinkle with some flaky sea salt while the bread is still hot, then eat as soon as possible.

BREAD & UNMISSABLES

Honey & Smoke Moroccan-inspired sourdough rolls

Makes 16 rolls

This is the bread we have served to almost every table at Honey & Smoke since the very first day we opened. It is the best I have ever created: soft yet ever so slightly crunchy, salty and comforting, and great for soaking up extra virgin olive oil and every last drop of sauce from the plate. Itamar warns customers not to fill up on bread so that they can enjoy the food to follow, but for many, it's a central part of the meal.

I wasn't planning to include this recipe, as these rolls demand time, effort and skill, but we are asked for it so often that I feel I simply must share it. Be warned: you will need a sourdough starter, which can take a couple of weeks (and isn't always successful), and shaping the very soft dough can be a source of heartache too. Certainly I wouldn't recommend that you tackle this unless you are a relatively capable baker.

If you already have a sourdough starter, by all means use it; if not, follow the recipe below to create a 'mother dough' just as we did 5 years ago. You must use organic ingredients to ensure there are plentiful bacteria spores to form your sourdough.

For the mother dough

500 g / 1 lb 2 oz organic raisins

1 lt / 1¾ pints water

2 kg / 4 lb 8 oz organic flour (added over 2 weeks)

Place the raisins and water in a large jar, cover with a cloth (not a lid) and leave for 3 days at room temperature.

Strain the water into a large bowl (discard the raisins or use them for cooking). Add 500 g / 1 lb 2 oz of the flour to the water, stir well to combine, and pour back into the jar. Cover with the cloth again and leave at room temperature for 24–36 hours.

Discard half the mixture and pour the remainder into a large bowl. Stir 500 g / 1 lb 2 oz flour into the remainder, along with as much water as necessary to form a very thick paste. Return to the jar, re-cover with the cloth and leave for 24–36 hours again.

Repeat this process twice more to use up all the flour. You should now have a bubbling sourdough starter that smells nice and funky, ready to use in this recipe (or, indeed, in any other recipe that calls for sourdough).

Store the starter in a closed jar in the fridge. Every 48 hours or so remove 300 g / 10½ oz of the starter (you can discard this or bake with it) and feed the remainder with 200 g / 7 oz flour and 100 ml / 3½ fl oz water. Allow to rest at room temperature for 2 hours before returning to the fridge. Your starter will improve and develop over time, as long as you remember to feed it regularly.

For the rolls

450 ml / 15¾ fl oz warm water

90 ml / 3¼ fl oz vegetable oil

600 g / 1 lb 5 oz strong bread flour

30 g / 1 oz spelt flour

30 g / 1 oz sugar

30 g / 1 oz salt

600 g / 1 lb 5 oz mother dough (see left)

For shaping

1 lt / 1¾ pints cold water

100 g / 3½ oz course semolina

To finish

olive oil for brushing

2 tbsp fennel seeds, roughly crushed

coarse grey sea salt (*sel gris*)

Place the warm water, vegetable oil, flours, sugar, salt and mother dough in this order in the bowl of a large electric mixer with a hook attachment and knead on a low speed for 3 minutes. Scrape down the sides and base of the bowl to make sure you incorporate all the flour, then increase the speed to medium-high and continue kneading for 10 minutes until you have a smooth, shiny, rather loose dough. Cover and leave to rest for 4 hours at room temperature.

Turn the dough out onto a clean work surface and use a pastry cutter to divide into 16 pieces, each about 110 g / 4 oz. The dough will be super-soft but don't worry, that's the secret to producing a really fluffy texture.

The rolls can be tricky to shape, but practice makes perfect – you'll get the knack. Set the cold water in a bowl and put the semolina in a wide dish nearby. Use the water to moisten your hands before lifting each dough blob. Fold the dough in on itself until it forms a ball. Pop the smooth, rounded side (what will be the upper crust) into the semolina, then flip over to coat the rougher seam-side too (where the dough was folded). Lift the ball out carefully and lay seam-side down on a baking tray, allowing 5cm/2inches between each roll. Leave for 2–2½ hours until proved.

Heat your oven to 220°C/200°C fan/gas mark 7. If you have a wood-burning oven, great; if not, use your kitchen oven with a baking stone, if you have one. Place the tray of rolls in the oven, spray them generously with water and bake for 12 minutes. Open the oven, rotate the tray 180 degrees to ensure an even bake and spray again. Reduce the temperature to 200°C/180°C fan/gas mark 6 and bake for another 10 minutes before removing.

To finish, place the rolls upside down on the grill for 30–40 seconds, then flip them over and grill for another 20 seconds. Brush the tops with olive oil, sprinkle with the fennel seeds and salt, and serve.

Fire-top *knafe*

Fills a 28 cm / 11 inch frying pan (or a *knafe* pan, if you own one)

There aren't many Middle Eastern recipes for sweet things cooked on the fire. The tradition is only to serve fresh or dried fruit to end a meal, or maybe tiny, very sugary *baklavas*, mini doughnuts or halva, if you want to spoil your guests. Fire-top *knafe* is an exception to this rule. This combination of desiccated *kadaif* pastry, stringy cheese, rich syrup and a hint of smoke was celebrated in Jordan more than in any other place we visited. I didn't understand why the pastry was desiccated until I got back to London, started experimenting, and jammed one mincer after another with fresh pastry. The heat in Jordan dries the pastry, making it brittle and requiring a new method to make it delicious again. You will need to open a packet of fresh *kadaif* pastry and leave it on a tray in a warm room for a day or two to dry out completely. You can make the sugar syrup and *kadaif* crust in advance, so you just need to prepare the filling and cook this on the day of serving.

For the sugar syrup

400 g / 14 oz granulated sugar

230 ml / 8¼ fl oz water

a squeeze of lemon juice

2 tsp orange blossom water (you can use more or less, to taste)

For the crust

375 g / 13 oz *kadaif* dough, air-dried till crisp

100 ml / 3½ fl oz sugar syrup (the rest is poured over the cooked *knafe*)

45 ml / 1½ fl oz water

100 g / 3½ oz melted ghee

For the filling

250 g / 9 oz fresh mozzarella

250 g / 9 oz hard mozzarella (the stuff you can grate)

To cook and serve

30 g / 1 oz melted ghee to brush the pan

ground pistachios to garnish (optional)

Combine the sugar, water and lemon juice for the syrup in a medium saucepan, set on the BBQ over a high heat and bring to the boil. Move to a low heat and let it simmer very gently for about 10 minutes. Remove from the heat and stir in the orange blossom water. You could, of course, prepare this on the stove if you prefer.

Break up the dried *kadaif* pastry, then mince in a meat mincer or grind in a coffee grinder until you have a fine powder. Place in a bowl, pour over 100 ml / 3½ fl oz of sugar syrup, the water and the ghee, and mix till the pastry is well-coated and resembles cooked couscous. Bake in the oven at 170°C/150°C fan/gas mark 3–4 for 15 minutes, stirring every 5 minutes until dry and crumb-like, but still pale. Allow to cool and store in an airtight container until needed.

Drain the fresh mozzarella and roughly tear apart. Place in a bowl, roughly grate in the hard mozzarella and stir to combine.

Brush the base of your frying pan (or *knafe* pan) with the ghee. Set aside 4 tablespoons of the toasted pastry crumbs and press the rest into the base of the pan to form a crust. Spread the cheese mixture over the crust, leaving a 1 cm / 3/8 inch border uncovered around the edge. Set the pan over a mellow, low heat and cook for 10–12 minutes, rotating the pan every 2 minutes, until the outermost edge of the crust turns deep golden brown and the cheese has started to melt. Sprinkle the reserved crumbs over the melting cheese layer, cover, remove from the heat and leave to rest for 5 minutes. Then take a large plate that can easily fit the diameter of the frying pan and place it on top. Very carefully, holding the two together, flip them over so the *knafe* is on the plate. The cheese will now be the base, and the crispy crust will be on top. Douse with all the remaining sugar syrup, sprinkle with pistachios (if you wish) and serve hot.

Grilled stone fruits with rosemary and rose syrup

A dessert for 4–6

Summer's stone fruits react particularly well to being grilled: their sweetness intensifies in the heat and is countered by a hint of smoke. If you have roses in full bloom when making this dish, it would be a shame not to use the fragrant petals to make the syrup to bathe the fruit. Waiting until the BBQ has reduced in heat to a lovely smoulder is key here, making this dish perfect to round off the evening. It is delicious served hot with cold vanilla ice cream or, once cooled, with sour cream and some shortbread.

4 peaches and/or nectarines

6 loquats and/or apricots

8 small plums

20–24 cherries

a few sprigs of rosemary

For the syrup

70 g / 2½ oz sugar

50 ml / 1¾ fl oz water

petals from 2 organic roses (or 1 tbsp rose water)

2 thin slices of lemon

You can either place all the fruit on the grill in one go, turning occasionally, and take them off as they cook, or start with the peaches as they will need the longest (about 6–8 minutes), then add the apricots (5–6 minutes), then the plums (about 2–3 minutes) and finally the cherries for just a minute to loosen their flavour and juices. Add the whole sprigs of rosemary to the grill for a few seconds to enliven the oils and then put the grilled fruit and rosemary in a serving bowl.

Mix the sugar with the water, rose petals and lemon slices in a small saucepan and bring to a boil on the side of the grill. Allow to cook for 3 minutes, then carefully pour over the fruit.

BREAD & UNMISSABLES

HOW TO BBQ

General guidelines for starting a fire

Where to start

Most of the recipes in this book were tried on a simple grill or BBQ: a cooking rack on top of a metal vessel, usually with high sides to contain the burning charcoal or wood and a couple of air holes. You can splurge on a super-stylish Green Egg ceramic contraption or buy a cheapo disposable BBQ tray, and get amazing results from either. You could even use a small fire pit, encircled with stones to contain the fire; just balance a metal rack across the stones or set a metal stand directly over the embers.

Honestly, we just cook on whatever is around, from the flimsiest little metal tray to the fanciest 3-tiered adjustable-height grill. Some of the recipes (the ones in which the food bakes in the embers) can be recreated in a wood-burning stove, and once we even ended up using an old wheelbarrow as a BBQ, and that worked just fine too.

The point is, use a heat-resistant metal container, fill it with fuel (more to come on that soon), put a metal rack or grill on top, and you are set.

The equipment

Tongs are the most useful bit of kit. They can be used to shift fuel to the exact location you need it, lift food on and off the grill, and keep you a safe distance from the fire. Buy a pair of long tongs, ideally with wooden or silicone handles that won't heat up too much if left close to the fire.

A long BBQ fork is helpful too. Use it to spear a halved onion (cut from root to tip, skin left on) and rub the cut surface over the grill rack to clean it, then dip in a little vegetable oil and rub over the rack again to oil it, so the food doesn't stick. The fork can also be used with the tongs to help when turning larger items on the fire.

A metal brush can be used to clean the grill. Look for one with really thick metal bristles and a wooden handle so it doesn't heat up too much. (We go through these at an alarming rate at Honey & Smoke.)

A fan will help you create air flow when starting the fire and if you need to increase the heat while you cook. A rush of oxygen works wonders in enlivening a flame. You can use any thick piece of cardboard or a hand-held fan, or even an old hairdryer (obviously the latter will only work if you're in easy reach of an electric socket).

Skewers, metal or wooden, are great on the BBQ. They come in many different sizes and thicknesses. Wide, flat ones are traditionally used for minced meat kebabs, as they provide structure, helping the kebabs stay in one piece during cooking, as well as conducting heat through the mixture. Thin metal skewers work best with delicate foods like prawns, or diced fish or chicken breast. The long ones with a decorative twist at the end are good for grilling vegetables and chunks of meat, as the twist helps the food stay in place. In general terms, we find that metal skewers are better than wooden ones, as they conduct heat to cook the food inside too, but if you can only get your hands on wooden ones, make sure to soak them in plenty of cold water for a few hours before using, or they will simply burn away on the grill.

A long-handled spatula can be very useful for turning more delicate items like fish kofta, slices of cheese, soft vegetables and fruit, which otherwise might break up if handled with tongs. Sliding a spatula underneath them enables you to flip them gently in one piece.

Grill baskets or grill cages are made of two hinged sheets of wire mesh and a handle. The two sheets are secured together with a latch to create a flat cage for holding whole fish (the skin tends to stick to the BBQ if grilled directly), small items like chicken wings and livers, and vegetables like green beans, asparagus and mushrooms that might otherwise fall through onto the coals. Ideally brush the inner surface of the wire mesh on both sides with vegetable oil before placing anything in the basket, to ensure that nothing sticks.

A large, perforated metal tray or metal colander is not a necessity by any means, but it is a very useful piece of kit for roasting nuts or seeds over the fire, or for creating a makeshift smoker (simply put the food inside, cover with a lid and place over the fire in the very early stages while it is producing lots of smoke).

The fuel

Charcoal is the simplest, least-smoky, most common fuel for home grilling, and is relatively easy to light. There are plenty of varieties, some with fancy names, provenance and burning times. It is worth trying to source environmentally sustainable charcoal (and wood) locally, so check on the internet to find your nearest supplier and ask for recommendations. In the Middle East charcoal tends to be produced from olive, citrus and pine wood, while in the UK it is more likely to be native oak, ash, hazel or beech. You can, of course, experiment to compare different aromas, burning times and the heat yields, but the chances are that, unless you use it daily (or run a grill restaurant), you will buy what is available, and it will work just fine. In Honey & Smoke, because of necessity and city laws, we use long-burning, low-smoke-emitting, industrially compressed charcoal. It isn't romantic sounding but it helps reduce London's air pollution a little, and the food still tastes great.

Dry wood of any type will produce a more aromatic and smoky fire than charcoal, and aromatic smoke is what you need to impart extra flavour to your food. I once read a list of all the varieties, their smoke and the foods they work with best. It was an amazingly informative list… and one that I will never use. You might occasionally splash out and buy some dried maple or citrus wood at a garden centre, but otherwise, unless you have a fruit orchard or are burning huge quantities, you will probably just use the same wood as for a wood-burning stove, or whatever you can pick up at the supermarket. Whatever you use, make sure it is really dry so it catches well.

A combination of charcoal and wood is our preference. It is easy to light, creates a stable, aromatic fire, and still taps into the primal fascination of watching a log of wood smouldering away.

How much fuel you need varies because each fire burns differently. It also depends on how much cooking you intend to do. As a general rule allow at least: 5 kg / 11 lb charcoal for a purely charcoal fire; 8 kg / 18 lb wood (6–8 logs) for a purely wood fire; and 2–3 kg / 4–7 lb charcoal plus 4–5 logs for a combination fire.

Starting a fire

Kindling is a necessity. Paper, thick cardboard, dry pine cones (if you can find them) and old egg boxes all work well. When using wood, bark catches the best, so if you can find nice chunks of wood with a cracking bark around, start with these. This is especially true of silver birch, the papery bark of which is a natural fire starter. We never use fire-lighters at work or at home. We are sure that it can't be good for the environment to burn these condensed chemical tablets, plus their horrible-smelling smoke can sometimes taint the food on the grill.

Patience is a must. It takes time to start a decent fire, and more time to feed it and let it mellow until it is ready to cook on. As a rule of thumb you should start it about 30–40 minutes before you want to cook; allow 15–20 minutes for the fire to catch well and flame up, and another 15–20 minutes for it to burn down and mellow. Once it is going, occasional smaller feeds with wood or charcoal are easier to monitor.

A fire chimney is a wide metal pipe with a large handle, and holes at the base and along the side to allow air flow. Chimneys are cheap, widely available and hands down the easiest and fastest way to start a fire. You stuff a whole load of kindling into the base of the pipe, add charcoal on top, and light the kindling through one of the holes in the side. You can then leave it for about 15–20 minutes, and with no effort at all you should have plenty of glowing coals. Scatter them over the base of the grill and feed with more charcoal or wood. Don't cover the coals too densely as you want the new fuel to catch well and burn off. Allow to mellow until there are no visible flames and the coals look slightly grey with a red glow.

A little 'teepee' or pyramid of fuel and kindling will help get things going if you don't have a fire chimney. The main thing to remember here is to leave plenty of gaps for air to travel through. Start by making a wide base of dry wood or bigger pieces of charcoal. Place some crumpled-up paper balls or stacked egg cartons in the middle, then build up your kindling teepee around them, overlaying and criss-crossing the fuel, with some more paper crumpled up in a couple of spots. Remember that heat always goes up, so the higher you can make your kindling structure, the better. Apply a match to the paper in the centre and let it catch. We have seen people wrapping the sides of the teepee in aluminium foil to create an open-topped tent to help it catch light faster. This is effective, if rather wasteful, but if you are really hungry, then you may want to give it a go.

A fan will help the air flow, giving the fire the oxygen it needs. You can use a thick piece of cardboard or plastic to fan the flames, or a little hand-held fan, or even an old hair dryer (although you will need access to electricity for this, so not an option if you're cooking in the wild). Take care not to blow embers away or you may start a fire in a different place than intended.

Mellowing the fire, ready to grill

Once the fire is well-lit, you need to mellow it down. This is the most beautiful stage, when the embers and wood are glowing red. Spread them out over the base of the grill or fire pit, feed them with some more wood or charcoal, and create a flat bed of heat. Test the temperature by holding your hand about 10 cm / 4 inches above the coals; within 3–4 seconds it should be so hot that you need to pull your hand away. You are now ready to cook.

Essentially, you treat your grill as a stove, dividing it into thirds. Use a metal scraper or tongs to pile the fuel high at one side of the grill – this is your high-heat zone. Create a full but rather lower layer of charcoal in the middle – this is your medium-heat zone. The other third of the grill is your low-heat zone, and should have a sparse scattering of charcoal, possibly with a slow-smouldering log of wood for smoke and flavour. You should be able to feel the difference in heat between the three zones when you hold your hand 10 cm / 4 inches above them: you will need to pull it away after 3–4 seconds over the hot zone, after 6–8 seconds over the medium zone, and after about 10 seconds over the low zone. Please remember this is only a rough guide – different people have different heat thresholds. Another way to check is with a piece of baking paper held over each section: it should catch fire around the time that you would have whipped your hand away.

Other practicalities

Clean the rack/grill before you cook anything on it. A halved onion (cut root to tip) pronged on a BBQ fork and dipped in vegetable oil is a really good tool for removing debris from the last time you grilled, or you could use a metal-bristled brush. Any remaining food particles will burn off in the heat of the fire, so you don't need to worry about cross-contamination. Don't wash the grill with water, as you want to build a black patina which will form a non-stick surface over time; in other words you want to season it, as you would a cast-iron pan.

Let the food char before you start prodding and turning it. If you try and flip a cut of meat or fish (or even a sliced vegetable) too early, it will stick to the grill. If it has had a chance to cook a little and form a 'crust', it should come off easily. So don't fight the food or try and peel it off before it is ready; just give it a couple more minutes.

Start grilling the biggest cuts first, finishing them off slowly over the low-heat zone while you cook the smaller, thinner items on the high-heat zone. This way you should be able to coordinate your timings so that everything is ready together.

Keep grilled items warm if you are cooking a large amount of food in batches. Either pop it into a low-heat oven (if you have one nearby) or place it on a covered tray by the side of the grill to keep it warm and delicious while you cook the rest of the meal.

Cover the food while it is resting. We don't have many recipes for larger cuts in this book as they aren't traditional BBQ fare in the Middle East, but if you are cooking a big hunk of meat, a whole chicken or a very thick steak, pop a cover over it to retain the heat while it cooks and then rests. Some BBQs come with an in-built lid, but any large metal dome, bowl or deep tray will do the trick.

Hot-smoke your food on the grill for added flavour. You can either set it over a wood fire as it is being lit and producing lots of smoke, or add a large handful of wood chippings to an already-mellow charcoal fire to achieve the same effect. Put the food in a perforated tray or metal colander, then cover with a tight-fitting lid or aluminium foil and place on a high rack above the fire to capture the smoke.

Build a home-made smoker to cold-smoke food. This can even be done indoors. Simply place the contents of 1 tea bag or 1 heaped teaspoon of dried tea leaves, a couple of spoonfuls of sugar, whole dried spices (try cinnamon bark, bay leaves, coriander seeds or cumin seeds) and wood chippings in the base of an old baking tray that you no longer use for cooking, and set light to them with matches or a piece of smouldering charcoal. Place a perforated tray or wire rack on top of the smouldering aromatics, carefully cover with aluminium foil to seal and leave to smoke for anything from 5 to 40 minutes, depending on what you are smoking and the intensity of flavour you want. Detailed guidelines are set out in the recipes where we use this technique.

Now go forth and channel your inner caveman. Start a fire and feel a sense of achievement. Hopefully you too will fall in love with the art of cooking over fire.

Index

Index

Thank you

A place is only as memorable, only as beautiful, as the people you meet there, and that is what this book is about. It owes its existence to all the people we encountered on our travels; some are mentioned in these pages, but most are not. Our first and foremost thanks are to those we met on the way whose names we can't remember or never knew.

In Pavilion we are grateful to Polly, Helen, Cara, Kom and the team for allowing us to go on these jolly adventures and for helping us realise this *fata morgana*, and to Luigi for setting us up.

This book turned out to be a much bigger, more complex project than we ever envisaged. Through a twist of good fate we got to join forces again with Elizabeth Hallett as our editor and thank God that we did. Without her swooping in, whipping us into shape, encouraging us, picking up all the different threads and weaving them into coherence, there would not be a book, or certainly not a good one.

Bryony Nowell – it is worth making books just for the sheer pleasure of working with you and reading your little notes on our copy, which make our heart and our copy sing.

To Dave Brown at Ape, who came to meet us under the murals in Morley college as we were covered in clay dust; you got a wonky pot and we got the book of our dreams – not a bad trade off. We hope we can do this again.

Patricia Niven we thank twice: first for the creative vision she brought to this book, her curious gaze, her love of plastic chairs and sickly street cats, her amazing talent for opening doors and hearts, and her command of the sunlight; and second for being the best companion imaginable, always pleasant, always game, always hungry. We could not have done this with anybody else. (We hope we weren't too painful.) The pictures in this book – and the ones that didn't make it in – are a record of us in our happiest moments, when traveling was carefree. How lucky we are to have had that, and to have had it

recorded by someone as gifted as Patsy.

A big thank you to everyone who kept the home fires burning in London while we were gallivanting around chasing smoke. The teams in our restaurants are ever-changing, but the love and care is constant. Thanks to the four pillars on which the company stands: Julia Chodubska, Rachael Gibbon, Louisa Cornford and Inbal Yeffet Cannon. We can and should write whole books about how great each of you are. One day we will.

To our parents, siblings, nieces, nephews and friends who came, cooked, ate and gave their time, their homes and gardens, bits of their sanity and bits of advice. You made this book; you make our life.

To our guests in the restaurants, shoppers at the deli, readers of our columns and books, the food-writing community and our online community – it is all thanks to you and for you. We hope we are worthy.